D0140668

MARTIN S. REMLAND | TIMOTHY J. BROWN | KAY NEAL

West Chester University of Pennsylvania

University of Wisconsin-Oshkosh

second edition

Argumentation *and* DEBATE

A PUBLIC SPEAKING APPROACH

Kendall Hunt

publishing company

Cover and all interior images © Shutterstock, Inc.

Kendall Hunt
publishing company

www.kendallhunt.com
Send all inquiries to:
4050 Westmark Drive
Dubuque, Iowa 52002

Copyright © 2007, 2014 by Kendall/Hunt Publishing Company

ISBN 978-1-4652-5202-9

All rights reserved. No part of this publication may be reproduced, stored in a retrieval system, or transmitted, in any form or by any means, electronic, mechanical, photocopying, recording, or otherwise, without the prior written permission of the copyright owner.

Printed in the United States of America

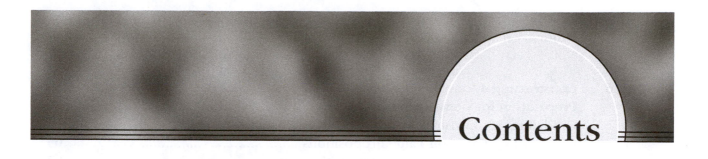

Contents

Preface

We began this project because of our desire for a textbook on argumentation and debate that addresses the needs of students with no prior experience in formal debate, limited experience in public speaking, and little or no plans to compete in speech and debate tournaments. Of course, this is not to say that students with some speech and debate experience who may be thinking about joining the forensics team on their campus will not benefit from this book. In fact, our streamlined coverage of the basics and our public speaking approach will help all students develop or enhance their argumentation and debate skills in analysis, research, case construction, presentation, refutation, and cross-examination. For some readers, our book may serve as a springboard to more inquiry into the theory and practice of argumentation and debate. For these readers, we recommend a number of excellent books that offer more in-depth or specialized coverage than that provided here (see Appendix C for a list of books).

Our approach to argumentation and debate stresses basic public speaking skills such as managing speech anxiety, doing research, understanding your audience, preparing a speech, speaking with limited notes, and so on. But the skills needed for argumentation and debate also include attacking and defending arguments, accurate and comprehensive note taking, case construction, and cross-examination.

Chapter 1 introduces our public speaking approach and highlights the many benefits of learning the skills of argumentation and debate. Chapters 2, 3, and 4 focus on *argumentation*: analyzing arguments, recognizing fallacies, and using and testing evidence. Chapters 5, 6, and 7 focus on *debate* and include the topics of analyzing debate propositions, and constructing and presenting cases for and against propositions. We conclude the book with two application chapters: Chapter 8 discusses different educational formats and Chapter 9 discusses argumentation and debate in different professional contexts.

We are delighted that Kendall Hunt agreed to support this project and appreciate the guidance and encouragement we have received from our editors, Leah Schneider and Sara McGovern, with whom we hope to continue working in the future.

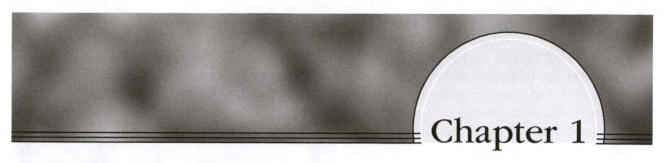

Chapter 1

Introduction to Argumentation and Debate

CHAPTER OUTLINE

KEY TERMS

Argumentation
Audience Analysis
Claim
Critical Thinking
Culture
Cultural Belief
Debate
Demographics

Ethos
Extemporaneous Speaking
Identification
Logos
Maslow's Hierarchy of Needs
Pathos
Proof
Rhetoric

We live in an information age when we are bombarded with argument and debate on issues that impact public policy, social and cultural norms, and individual attitudes and beliefs. A historical example includes the terrorist attacks of 9/11. In response to the terrorist attacks, President Bush took military action against Afghanistan for sheltering the mastermind of 9/11 and leader of al-Qaeda, Osama bin Laden. Governments around the world largely supported the American invasion of Afghanistan.

1

When the Bush administration, however, shifted its focus to Iraq, claiming that Iraq was part of the larger war on terror, it caused much more international and national criticism, debate, and protests for and against an invasion of Iraq.[1] The arguments and justifications for going to war, such as Saddam Hussein posed an imminent threat to the United States and the region, Iraq possessed weapons of mass destruction, Hussein was involved with 9/11, and Iraq harbored terrorists, were fiercely debated leading up to and after the invasion.

Another argument that made the American invasion of Iraq even more debatable was the idea of a preemptive war—that the United States had the right to defend itself against countries that were a perceived threat. The idea was controversial because never before had the United States launched a preemptive war. Nevertheless, the conflict in Iraq and the larger war on terror continues to dominate the national political discussion.[2]

The war in Iraq also highlights the vital role of argumentation and debate in our society today. Argumentation and debate is a dynamic process where ideas are accepted, challenged, and/or rejected depending on the

Democratic societies are characterized by argument and debate on public issues.

attitudes and beliefs of the audience. Certain arguments will resonate with audiences while being rejected by others, as the war in Iraq demonstrates.

The Iraq example, however, represents only one of many debates that shape our public policy. Our political, legal, educational, religious, and organizational systems all use argumentation to create policies and make decisions, but argumentation and debate is not limited to these contexts. We engage in argumentation every day whether we are choosing between cell phone plans, convincing a friend to loan us money, or even deciding on a major. All of these examples, national and individual, legal and social, exemplify the crucial role of argumentation in our society.

WHAT IS ARGUMENTATION AND DEBATE?

Although argumentation and debate is essential to how we make decisions, form opinions, and justify attitudes and beliefs, the tendency is for individuals to perceive argumentation and debate in an unfavorable way. When most people think of argumentation and debate, they think of an "argument" in which two or more people are engaged in a passionate disagreement with raised voices, angry assertions, and maybe even physical violence. While an argument might include these actions, argumentation and debate are quite different. We define these terms next.

Definition of Argumentation

Argumentation consists of explicit or implicit messages that are supported with evidence and reasoning. As suggested by our definition, argumentation involves two parts. First, the explicit or implicit message of an argument is referred to as a claim. A **claim** is a statement asserted to be true. Second, any claim or statement needs to be accompanied by evidence and reasoning. The evidence and reasoning that support a claim represents the **proof** (or grounds) in the argument. A speaker needs some proof in order to "show" how the claim makes sense, is logical and reasonable. Furthermore, whether an argument is successful or not depends on whether the proof (or grounds) provides good reasons for the audience to accept.[3]

For example, the evidence the Bush Administration used to support the claim that Saddam Hussein was a threat to the United States and the Middle East was that Hussein possessed weapons of mass destruction (WMDs). When Secretary of State Colin Powell appeared before the United Nations to argue this claim, Powell pointed to slides that suggested Iraq had bioweapons labs mounted on trucks. This "evidence," along with the fact that Saddam Hussein used chemical weapons during Iraq's 10-year war with Iran in the 1980s influenced many to believe that Hussein did have WMDs. Moreover, Hussein brought further suspicion upon himself by evicting U.N. inspectors from Iraq. After the U.S.-led invasion, it was not until after several attempts to find WMDs and congressional hearings into the claim that it was determined that the evidence Powell used in support of the invasion was incorrect.[4]

The previous example highlights several important concepts of argumentation that we will expand upon later on in this textbook. The claim (Hussein is a threat to the United States) and grounds (Hussein has WMDs) demonstrate two parts of Stephen Toulmin's model for argumentation, which is simply known as Toulmin's Model of Argumentation. The six parts of Toulmin's model include claim, grounds, warrant, backing, qualifier, and reservation. Each of these concepts will be explained in Chapter 2. Furthermore, the example underscores the importance of speakers being meticulous in finding and testing evidence that is used to support an argument. Using and testing evidence is addressed in Chapter 3. Meanwhile, how to construct an effective argument is explained in Chapter 6.

Definition of Debate

When individuals engage in argumentation, it occurs in a specific context and, when it follows established rules, it becomes a debate. A **debate** is a formal method of presenting arguments for and against a proposition. Depending on the type of debate, there are specific rules that individuals must follow and a sequence as to how the arguments are presented. Most debates can be categorized as professional or academic.

Debates that take place in a professional context often include a judge, audience, or group that has the power to make a binding decision on a proposition. Examples of professional debates include judicial debates (that take place in a courtroom), parliamentary debate (that occurs in legislative bodies such as Congress), and organizational debate (that uses Robert's Rules of Order to make group decisions). We discuss debate in professional contexts in Chapter 9.

Meanwhile, academic debates take place in secondary and higher education where a judge or audience does not make a binding decision but can pick a winner of the debate. Unlike professional debates, academic debates focus on providing an educational experience for the participants. Typically, academic debate takes place in a Forensics (Speech) Tournament where students compete against one another by following rules, such as the National Debate Tournament (NDT) or the Cross Examination Debate Association (CEDA) rules. We discuss academic debate in Chapter 8.

THE NATURE OF ARGUMENTATION AND DEBATE

The study of argumentation is as ancient as the beginning of civilization. Throughout the world, myriad scholars and philosophers from different cultures practiced, developed, and studied how rhetoric was used to influence others in their developing societies. From ancient China with philosophers such as Confucius, to Native American cultures, to ancient Arabic civilization to African-American rhetoric, each culture developed and practiced different rhetorical traditions.[5] Although this list is not exhaustive, it demonstrates how different cultures developed various rhetorical practices that reflected their cultures. For this reason, we stress the importance of debaters investigating their audience to become familiar with the audience's cultural values and beliefs in order to effectively adapt a message to the audience. Our multicultural society makes it necessary for speakers to develop messages that can appeal to diverse audiences.[6] How speakers can do this (audience analysis), is discussed further at the end of this chapter.

Although the study of argumentation has many roots, most of western cultures' understanding and development of debate has been influenced by ancient Greece. In the city-states of ancient Greece, argumentation and debate was a central component of their democracy. Since our democracy emulated the ancient Greeks, we relied on many of their ideas and practices for presenting an argument.

Defining Rhetoric

Classical rhetoricians defined rhetoric as the art of persuasive speaking. The study and practice of public speaking, however, led to a wealth of knowledge beyond simply constructing a persuasive speech. The ancient Greeks contributed to the understanding of rhetoric's philosophical roots, its techniques and its effects, and its connections between language and knowledge.[7] Over time, the study of rhetoric became much more than the study of persuasive speaking, to include the investigation of symbolic communication. Thus, we define **rhetoric** as the use of symbols (verbal and nonverbal) to influence others.

Symbols are representations (such as words, pictures, or gestures) that stand for an abstract idea or concept by relationship or association. For example, a red heart (symbol) could be a representation for the abstract concept of *Valentine's Day* or *Love*. However, if the heart is ripped, the ripped heart could stand for the abstract concept, a *Broken Heart*. Not only does this example illustrate how symbols represent abstract ideas, it also demonstrates how the strategic manipulation of a symbol can construct a different meaning.

When an individual uses rhetoric in a debate, he or she has made choices to use, relate, and modify symbols to create a desired meaning and effect in the audience. This is the foundation of argumentation and debate that we discuss in this textbook.

Classifying Rhetorical Contexts

In studying how rhetoric constructs meaning, the ancient Greeks created a classification for the different types of contexts that influenced the individual's use of rhetoric. These three areas include the types of rhetoric, the audience, and the elements of a speech. These principles provide a starting point for understanding the context and nature of argumentation and debate.

The types of rhetoric categorize the various public speeches that a speaker can engage in: the legal or *forensic speech,* the political or *deliberative speech,* and the ceremonial or *epideictic speech.* The legal or forensic speech takes place in a courtroom and involves the judgment about a past action. The political or deliberative speech takes place in a legislative body. The deliberative speech is concerned with persuading people to a future action. The ceremonial or epideictic speech takes place during a public occasion. It takes place in the present, yet will reference the past and future. These classifications are important in understanding how the context oftentimes determines the speaker's effectiveness.

Meanwhile, not only does the context influence the effectiveness of the speech, but the audience does as well. Classical rhetoric focuses upon understanding the psychology of different kinds of individuals who might compose an audience. The effective speaker understands that individuals are motivated by their own self-interest. Audience analysis is necessary to understand these self-interests. Often the speaker attempts to link an individual's self-interests to larger societal motivations and cultural beliefs in order to create an effective message to persuade the group instead of attempting to meet each individual need (which would be more time consuming).

In addition, not only does the self-interest affect the rhetoric of a speech, so does the type of audience. Audience analysis also reveals whether the audience is primarily a supportive, neutral, or hostile audience toward the speaker's position. The type of audience affects the speaker's rhetorical strategy, whether the speaker's goal is to convince, reinforce, or change an attitude or belief of the audience.

Classical rhetoric also defined the elements of a speech. These elements help the speaker construct a message in addition to serving as a means for evaluating a speech. Classical rhetoric divided a speech into the following parts: invention—how the speaker creates the speech through the concepts of **ethos** (source credibility), **pathos** (emotion), and **logos** (logic); arrangement— the organization of the speech; style—the use of language; memory—how well the speaker has memorized the speech; and delivery—the use of voice and gesture to present the speech. With the exception of memory, the canons of rhetoric are still considered essential for a speaker attempting to make a speech along with providing a standard to evaluate a speech. Classical rhetoric has provided a standard that emphasizes logos over ethos or pathos due to the insistence that claims must be supported by evidence and reasoning.

In sum, argumentation and debate has a long history of study and practice. In reviewing the legacy of the ancient Greeks, we can see they have provided us with a foundation for understanding how we use rhetoric to construct meaning and influence audiences. Furthermore, their work forms the foundation for the study and practice of argumentation and debate.

THE VALUE OF ARGUMENTATION AND DEBATE

Argumentation and debate is important in our everyday lives because we are constantly sending and receiving messages along with interpreting, evaluating, accepting, and/or rejecting arguments. The more we are aware of contemporary issues and the argumentation that accompanies them, the more we are able to analyze and evaluate arguments on national, local, and personal issues. For this reason, the study of argumentation and debate is extremely valuable.

Critical Thinking

When we engage in argumentation, we are using critical thinking in determining whether we accept or reject arguments. In general, **critical thinking** is the ability to carefully and deliberately evaluate the logical relationships among ideas, claims, and arguments to judge their validity and/ or worth. Critical thinking is an active process that requires us to compare claims (in relation to our own ideas and others) in order to make a decision about the truth of an idea.

When individuals construct and present arguments, members of the audience use critical thinking to evaluate the arguments based upon their own beliefs and knowledge of the topic. This is another reason we emphasize the importance of audience analysis because the effectiveness of argumentation is based upon the speaker's ability to adapt the argument to the specific audience in order to have the audience contemplate and thus think critically about the argument.

Participating in a Democratic Society

When we engage in critical thinking and begin to understand the arguments and perspectives that are related to societal issues, we become more informed citizens who can engage in the democratic process. Being an informed citizen also means understanding and appreciating the primary institutions of a democratic society—political, legal, and organizational—and how these institutions use argumentation and debate to resolve issues and make decisions. The more we learn about issues, arguments, formats and contexts of argumentation and debate, the more informed we become and the more we can participate effectively in our democratic society.

Argumentation Skills

Another benefit of taking a class in argumentation and debate is to improve one's argumentation skills. Like any endeavor, the more you practice, the better you get. Argumentation skills, which include researching, analysis, case construction, public speaking, and critical listening, are desirable because they help us understand the practice of supporting and responding to arguments. They also help us appreciate how arguments relate to our own self-interests and those of our audience. In studying argumentation, we learn to construct convincing arguments and analyze the arguments of others.

Decision-Making

When we improve our skills for critical thinking and we are able to make and evaluate different types of arguments, it leads to better decision-making. How? Because when we use critical thinking skills and argumentation skills, we tend not to accept information at face value. Instead, we test arguments, challenge the evidence, and ask questions so that better decisions occur. This is especially true in groups. Group decisions tend to be more effective if the decision was tested and challenged before accepted and implemented. Argumentation helps both individuals and groups to reach better decisions.

Personal and Professional Growth

Finally, argumentation leads to personal and professional growth. When we are engaged in our democratic society in national, local, and personal issues, we help ourselves and our communities become better places. Often in our careers, we will have to make decisions, argue for positions/ideas, and support our ideas with evidence and reasoning. Those who become adept at argumentation tend to excel at decision-making, which leads to personal and professional growth.

Argumentation enhances discussion and decision-making which leads to personal and professional growth.

A PUBLIC SPEAKING PERSPECTIVE ON ARGUMENTATION

Up until this point, we have discussed how argumentation is an everyday communication event that has been studied and practiced over the centuries. Argumentation also improves our ability to think critically about information (and evaluate it) as we engage in interpreting messages, making sense of messages, and ultimately accepting or rejecting messages. In this process, it is sometimes overlooked *how* one communicates arguments to a specific individual or audience. Although we are not advocating style over substance, the presentation of an argument in a debate can greatly affect how the audience receives a message (we discuss this in Chapter 7).

Extemporaneous Speaking

For this reason, we take a public speaking approach to the discussion of argumentation and debate. Without adapting a well-constructed message to a specific audience that is delivered in an effective extemporaneous manner, the argument, no matter how much it is supported with evidence, will not be successful. **Extemporaneous speaking** means planning and preparing a speech ahead of time and delivering the speech from an outline or notes. Although it appears to the audience that the speaker has given the speech for the first time, the speaker prepared and practiced several times in advance. Extemporaneous speaking enables the speaker to combine the benefits of a formal speaking style (organization, preparation, planning) and an informal speaking style (conversational tone, spontaneity, and movement/gestures).

In addition, the advanced planning and preparation of the speech enables speakers to adapt and relate specific arguments to an immediate audience in the effort to reinforce, convince, or change an audience's attitudes and/or belief. Speaking extemporaneously enables speakers to engage the audience with their delivery (such as conversational tone, movement/gestures) and adapt their speech to a specific audience. These principles of extemporaneous speaking underline a public speaking approach to argumentation and debate that we expand on next.

Creating Identification

A public speaking approach to argumentation and debate emphasizes that the speaker must prepare a speech that is adapted to the immediate audience and delivered extemporaneously. Any argument improves when the speaker presents information in a prepared and conversational manner. The presentation of the argument should not be a race through information where the speaker is monotone, speaks quickly, or reads from notes or a manuscript. To the contrary, the speaker must involve the audience in the presentation by adapting arguments to the immediate audience and using eye contact, gestures, facial expressions, movement, and tone of voice to engage the audience and to maintain the audience's attention.

When speakers can adapt a message to an audience, it creates identification that makes the speech more effective in attempting to persuade the audience. In fact, influential scholar Kenneth Burke argued that for speakers to be successful, they have to create identification with the audience.[8] **Identification** is when the speaker creates a common bond with the audience. The more the audience can identify with the speaker the more likely the audience will accept the argument and, hence, accept the position of the speaker. The concept of identification is central to a public speaking approach to argumentation and debate.

In addition to identification, we address other aspects of public speaking that greatly enhance a speaker's performance in argumentation and debate throughout this textbook. In Chapter 4, we discuss the importance of research, how to find credible evidence, and how to test and evaluate evidence. In Chapter 6, we explain how to organize a speech through the use of an outline and we explain how outlining is vital in constructing an effective speech. In Chapter 7, we discuss how to present an argument effectively and how to deal with speech anxiety.

We believe that a public speaking approach to argumentation and debate is crucial for creating effective arguments in a debate. In essence, a public speaking approach engages members of the audience and invites them to think critically about arguments that were adapted specifically to their attitudes and/or beliefs. Next we discuss how audience analysis is essential to a public speaking approach to argumentation and debate.

ARGUMENTATION AND AUDIENCE ANALYSIS

Among the many ideas from classical rhetoric that have survived the test of time is the idea that public speaking is an audience-centered process, which means all planning, research, and preparation must be directed at a specific audience if the speaker is to be effective. If the speaker does not relate the topic to the audience, the speech, no matter how well constructed or delivered it is, will not be very persuasive.

For example, consider a debate on the topic of immigration. A speaker providing argumentation for building a fence along the United States and Mexican border would be more effective if she can illustrate how illegal immigration affects her immediate audience. In making the argument, the speaker can cite evidence documenting the number of illegal immigrants and quotations from law enforcement, explaining how the current policy is not working. However, without explaining to the audience how immigration affects the audience's interests, the argument is probably going to be unsuccessful. This brief example illustrates how all public speaking begins with audience analysis. **Audience analysis** is discovering vital information about an audience in order to adapt a specific message to meet the needs of the audience. Audience analysis includes determining the audience's attitudes, demographics, needs, and situational factors.

Attitudes

Classical rhetoric emphasized the importance for speakers to discover the attitudes of the audience in order to create an effective message. This principle is still true today as audience analysis is necessary to understand the attitudes of the audience. A query to the audience that includes a series of questions about their attitudes and beliefs toward immigration would provide a starting point for understanding where the audience stands on the issue. Based upon the responses of the individuals in the audience, the speaker would be able to identify whether the audience is supportive, neutral, or hostile (or a combination thereof). The type of audience affects the speaker's rhetorical strategy whether the speaker's goal is to convince, reinforce, or change an attitude of belief of the audience.

For example, if the speaker discovered the audience was primarily a hostile group, the speaker's goal might be to convince the audience that the current system is not working and show how the situation affects the audience, and not to change the audience's attitude toward building a fence. This example highlights that discovering the attitudes of the audience by identifying its type is very beneficial for speakers. In this case, if the speaker assumed that the audience would "objectively" hear her argument and prepared to change the audience's attitude, the argument (although well-constructed and prepared) would be dismissed by the listeners.

Demographics

The **demographics** of the audience refer to the characteristics of the audience. The demographics of the audience can help the speaker make inferences toward the audience's interests. Some of the most common demographics include (but are not limited to) culture, ethnicity, gender, age,

Understanding the expectations, needs, and interests of a diverse audience is vital in constructing effective messages.

educational level, economic status, religious beliefs, political identification, and marital status. As we live in a multicultural society, it is only appropriate to briefly explain how culture and cultural beliefs can impact how a speaker adapts a message to an audience.

Culture can be defined as the traditions, beliefs, values, and practices that are passed down from generation to generation. A person's culture is an important demographic because culture serves as an implicit lens in which individuals construct, interpret, and attribute meaning. Culture can impact what we accept as evidence, what we consider a logical argument, and what we accept as truth.

Scholar Bell Hooks explained how behaviors and communication styles in one culture could have a different (and often negative meaning) in another. For example, Hooks discussed that in Asian-American culture, value is placed on pausing and thinking before speaking, which can be perceived by the dominant culture as being "slow" and "unsure." Meanwhile, African-American conversation is often defined by direct and loud conversation that can be interpreted by the dominant culture as "hostile."[9] In addition, some cultures value presenting information in a linear organizational pattern, while others favor more narrative or nonlinear communication styles.[10] These brief examples illustrate why it is important to know how a person's culture can impact the type of argument and how the argument is presented to the audience.

The cultural belief of the audience is another component of culture that cannot be overlooked by speakers. Each culture has cultural beliefs that also influence what arguments and evidence are accepted or rejected by the audience. A **cultural belief** is what a majority of individuals in a culture believe is true. For example, African Americans and whites tend to have differing beliefs toward law enforcement. African Americans tend to focus on how law enforcement treats the individual, who is formed from a long history of mistrust of, and abuse by, the police of African Americans. In contrast, whites tend to focus on the individual's behavior and the punishment of the individual because whites tend to trust the police.[11] For speakers, this information can influence the type of evidence used to support an argument. For example, an African-American audience would be more likely to question evidence that came from law enforcement (especially testimony), whereas a white audience would more likely not question the evidence as much.

Oftentimes, cultural beliefs can be influenced by factors such as a culture's orientation toward the following: individualism or collectivism, the value placed on the past, present, or future, and its ideals for success, fairness, and generosity. For example, individualist cultures place expectations on individuals to make their own way in society. Arguments that reinforce the idea that individuals are solely responsible for their welfare will resonate with these audiences. Meanwhile, collectivism suggests a group orientation. Arguments that emphasize the needs of the group over individual needs would resonate with these audiences. There are many cultural beliefs that influence our attitudes and beliefs.[12] We raise these examples to highlight how culture and cultural beliefs influence the perception and attitudes of audiences. Speakers have to be aware of, identify, and understand these cultural differences in order to appeal to a multicultural audience.

Audience Needs

Much like cultural beliefs, audiences also have individual self-interests or needs that speakers can appeal to in order to create identification with the audience. Appealing to audience needs is another way for speakers to adapt arguments to an audience. In addition, these needs that individuals have can be combined into specific categorizes often referred to as Maslow's Hierarchy of Needs.[13] **Maslow's Hierarchy of Needs** is based on the idea that individuals have specific desires and wants, which are arranged hierarchically and must be satisfied. According to Maslow, once basic needs are met then individuals can move on to satisfy higher level needs. These needs include:

- *Physical Needs*—the need for food, water, shelter, sleep, and air.
- *Safety Needs*—the need to have a sense of comfort, security, protection, and stability.
- *Belonging and Love Needs*—the need to be accepted, approved, and connected to others.
- *Esteem Needs*—the need for self-worth that comes from achievement and recognition.
- *Self-Actualization*—the need for self-fulfillment; to live up to one's potential.

Speakers can adapt a message to an audience by appealing to a specific need that is held by the audience. For example, returning to the immigration debate, suppose the speaker's audience analysis revealed that 85% of the audience is concerned about the safety of the country regarding a terrorist attack. The speaker could use this knowledge to argue for tougher immigration laws and more enforcement of existing policies by appealing to the audience's need for safety. The speaker could argue that "closing" the border and returning illegal immigrants to their countries is a way to ensure the security and protection of the country from a potential terrorist attack.

Situational Factors

Another aspect of audience analysis that speakers need to be aware of is the situational factors that can greatly influence the planning and preparing of a speech. Some of the most common situational factors include the size of the audience, the occasion, the significance, and the time of the presentation. The size of the audience can influence whether the speaker needs to be more formal (speaking behind a podium with a microphone) with a large audience, or informal (being able to use movement) and interact with a smaller audience. The occasion, whether the speech is an academic or professional debate, will impact the rhetorical strategies used by the speaker. In addition, the significance of the debate, whether the decision is binding or nonbinding, will affect how the speaker prepares for the debate. Finally, the speaker should also be aware of the time of day the presentation takes place. An audience's attention span can vary depending on whether the presentation takes place in the morning, afternoon, or night. Also, the number of speakers the audience has listened to prior to the speaker's own speech should be taken into account when preparing for the presentation. Situational factors might seem insignificant but they are all are very important to be aware of when adapting a message to the audience.

Acquiring Information for Audience Analysis

We do not want to overlook how speakers can acquire information about their audience in order to create an effective message. There are many different ways that speakers can analyze an audience; one of the simplest is to create a survey or questionnaire to determine the attitudes, beliefs, and positions of the audience. Sometimes, a personal contact can provide the necessary information on the audience and the occasion in order for the speaker to meet the needs of the audience.

SUMMARY

This chapter provided an introduction to the study and practice of argumentation and debate. We began by defining the terms argumentation and debate and explained how argumentation and debate evolved over time, as demonstrated by the influence the ancient Greeks continue to have on our ideas for an effective speech. Furthermore, the study of argumentation and debate is valuable as it is a means for critical thinking, our participation in a democratic society, argumentation skills, and decision-making. We also discussed our public speaking approach to argumentation and debate in order for speakers to create effective presentations. We ended the chapter by explaining how audience analysis is central to a public speaking approach and how individuals can use audience analysis in their presentations.

NOTES

1   Powel, M. (2003, March 23). Around globe, protest marches; In N.Y., 200,000 take to streets. *The Washington Post*, p. A19; Stolberg, S. (2007, January 11). Bush's new strategy for Iraq risks confrontations on many fronts. *The New York Times*, p. A19; Whitelaw, K., & Mulrine, A. (2007, January 22). 4th and long. *U.S. News & World Report*, pp. 31–33.

2   Mulrine, A. (2013, July 22). Al Qaeda growing, but less focused on US, study finds. *The Christian Science Monitor*. Retrieved from http://search.proquest.com/docview/1411053283?accountid=14971; Seib, G. F. (2013, May 29). What hasn't changed in the war on terror. *Wall Street Journal*, p. A4.

3   Toulmin, S. (1976). *Knowing and acting* (p. 138). New York, NY: Macmillian.

4   Priest, D., & Pincus, W. (2004, October 7). U.S. "almost all wrong" on weapons; report on Iraq contradicts Bush administration claims. *The Washington Post*, AOI.

5   See Lipson, C., & Brinkley, R. (Eds.). (2004). *Rhetoric before and beyond the Greeks*. Albany, NY: SUNY Press; Jackson, R., & Richardson, E. (Eds.). (2003). *Understanding African American rhetoric*. New York, NY: Routledge.

6   See Chen, G.-M., & Starosta, W. (2001). *Foundations of intercultural communication*. Needham Heights, MA: Allyn and Bacon.

7   Bizzell, P., & Herzberg, B. (Eds.). (2001). *The rhetorical tradition* (pp. 1–7). Boston, MA: Bedford/St. Martin's.

8   See Burke, K. (1969). *A rhetoric of motives*. Berkeley: University of California Press. (Original work published 1950).

9   See Hooks, B. (2000). *Feminist theory: From margin to center* (2nd ed.). Cambridge, MA: South End.

10 See Orbe, M., & Harris, T. (2007). *Interracial communication*. Thousand Oaks, CA: SAGE.

11 See Huggins, C. M. (2012). Traffic stop encounters: Officer and citizen race and perceptions of police propriety. *American Journal of Criminal Justice, 37*(1), 92–110; Tonry, M. (2010). The social, psychological, and political causes of racial disparities in the American criminal justice system. *Crime & Justice, 39*, 273–312.

12 Martin, J., & Nakayama, T. (2012). *Intercultural communication in contexts* (6th ed.). New York, NY: McGraw-Hill.

13 See Maslow, A. (1954). *Motivation and personality*. New York, NY: Harper & Row.

Chapter 2

Developing and Testing Arguments

CHAPTER OUTLINE

KEY TERMS

Backing
Claim
Deductive Argument
Grounds
Independent Arguments
Inductive Argument
Interdependent Arguments
Qualifier
Reasoning by Analogy

Reasoning by Authority
Reasoning by Cause
Reasoning by Definition
Reasoning by Generalization
Reasoning by Sign
Reservation
Syllogism
Toulmin Model
Warrant

A few years ago, Philadelphia's ban on smoking, The Clean Indoor Air Worker Protection Law, went into effect. Individuals who violate the law in local eating and drinking establishments are subject to a $300 fine.[1] While Philadelphia's ban on smoking represents a shift in public sentiment away from the rights of smokers and private businesses in favor of the health and safety of the public, concerned citizens on both sides of the issue continue to raise serious and thought-provoking arguments for and against such bans. As we noted in the previous chapter, it is our responsibility as members of a democratic society to make decisions on matters of public policy, whether those policies affect the world, such as the war on terror, or our local communities, such as ordinances against smoking in public places. To meet this important responsibility, we need skills that allow us to participate fully and competently in the discussions and debates that affect our lives and the lives of others.

In Chapter 1, we introduced the concept of argumentation and noted that all arguments consist of a claim and support for that claim. In this chapter, we consider the importance of **reasoning**; that is, how a premise provides support for a claim. We begin with a discussion of how to analyze an argument, breaking it down into its basic parts. Then, we focus on recognizing and testing different types of arguments.

ANALYZING AN ARGUMENT

How do we "analyze" an argument? Put simply, we analyze something when we take it apart and study the parts. So, the first step in analyzing an argument is to take the argument apart, to separate the claim from the premise, and examine the basic parts or elements of the argument. Unfortunately, when people make arguments, whether in oral or written form, they rarely, if ever, label the parts for us. For instance, they don't tell us whether the argument is "inductive" or "deductive," an important distinction that determines how we should judge the strength of the argument; and quite often they don't even tell us what the "point" of the argument is (i.e., the claim). One characteristic of being a critical thinker is being able to do this kind of analysis.

Deductive and Inductive Arguments

All arguments contain a claim backed up by one or more premises, or reasons, which constitute the proof of the claim. For instance, a friend of Brian's, Gayle, tries to convince Brian to buy a plasma TV <u>because</u> they have a sharper picture than LCD TVs. In this case, we can take Gayle's argument apart as follows:

Claim: *You (Brian) should buy a plasma TV,* because_ . . .

Premise: *Plasma TVs have a sharper picture than LCD TVs*

Notice in the above argument, we presented the claim first and then the premise. The term "because" indicates the sequence: claim-premise. On the other hand, using the term "therefore" indicates the opposite sequence: premise-claim, as stated in the following:

Premise: *Plasma TVs have a sharper picture than LCD TVs,* therefore_ . . .

Claim: *You (Brian) should buy a plasma TV*

Of course, the claim in one argument can become the premise in another, and vice versa. For instance, the premise in the above argument becomes the *claim* in the following:

Claim: *Plasma TVs have a sharper picture than LCD TVs,* because . . .

Premise: *Consumer Reports says that plasma TVs have a sharper picture*

The relationship between a claim and a premise, which represents the reasoning in an argument, depends on whether the argument is deductive or inductive. In a **deductive argument**, the claim must follow from the premises. That is, if we accept the premises, we have to accept the claim. It is a logical necessity. In this sense, the claim in a deductive argument is either *valid* (we must accept it) or *invalid* (we don't have to accept it). We express these arguments in a distinct form known as a **syllogism**. To illustrate, consider the following:

Major premise: *All artists are creative*

Minor premise: *Ted is an artist*

Claim: *Ted is creative*

In this argument, called a ***categorical syllogism***, we must accept the claim if we accept the premises. As illustrated above, we begin with an initial premise (called the major premise) that a class of things (A) share a certain attribute (B), a secondary premise (called a minor premise) that something in particular (C) belongs to that class (A), followed by a claim that this thing (C) possesses the attribute (B). Thus, we can express the argument above as follows:

Major premise: *All A's are B*

Minor premise: *C is an A*

Claim: *C is B*

Two other common types of deductive arguments are disjunctive syllogisms and hypothetical syllogisms. A ***disjunctive syllogism*** expresses in the major premise an "either-or" relationship between two things that we assume are mutually exclusive (i.e., both cannot exist), and the argument takes the following form:

Major premise: *Either A exists or B exists*

Minor premise: *A exists*

Claim: *B does not exist*

Alternatively, in the minor premise one could assert that *A does not exist*, producing the claim that *B exists*, or one could assert in the minor premise that *B exists*, which leads to the claim that *A does not exist*. Here is an example of a disjunctive syllogism:

Major premise: *Either the Phillies won the game or they lost the game*

Minor premise: *The Phillies won the game*

Claim: *The Phillies didn't lose the game*

A ***hypothetical syllogism*** (also called a conditional syllogism) expresses an "if-then" relationship between things. The major premise assumes that the presence of one thing, called the antecedent (A), indicates the presence of another thing, referred to as the consequent (B). In a pure hypothetical syllogism, the premises and the claim express "if-then" relationships as a chain of events (i.e., if one thing happens, then another thing will happen). Here is an example of such an argument:

Major premise: *If A, then B*   *If you pass the test, you'll pass the course*

Minor premise: *If B, then C*   *If you pass the course, you'll graduate in June*

Claim: *If A, then C*   *If you pass the test, you'll graduate in June*

In a mixed hypothetical syllogism, only the major premise expresses an "if-then" relationship. There are two valid forms of this argument: (1) when the minor premise *affirms the antecedent*, and (2) when the minor premise *denies the consequent*:

Affirming the Antecedent

Major premise: *If A, then B*   *If it rains, the roof will leak*

Minor premise: *A*   *It is raining*

Claim: *B*   *The roof will leak*

Denying the Consequent

Major premise: *If A, then B*   *If it rains, the roof will leak*

Minor premise: *not B*   *The roof is not leaking*

Claim: *not A*   *It did not rain*

The practice of testing a deductive argument involves determining whether or not the claim follows logically from the premises, not whether or not the claim is true. For instance, in both hypothetical syllogisms above, the claims are valid but not necessarily true (i.e., that depends on whether the premises are true). Determining the probable truth of any claim is what we do when testing the strength of an **inductive argument**. In the next section, we discuss the most widely used method of analyzing inductive arguments.

The Toulmin Model of Argument

What are the basic parts of an inductive argument? Based on the work of British philosopher Stephen Toulmin, our analysis begins by isolating the **claim**, or conclusion in an argument.[2] Of course, a claim without a premise is not an argument, but merely an *__unsupported assertion__*. Using the Toulmin model, we call the premise the **grounds** for the claim (also called the ***data***). Consider the argument we introduced in Chapter 1, used by the Bush Administration to justify the war in Iraq: *Saddam Hussein is a threat to the United States* because *he has weapons of mass destruction (WMDs)*. This argument clearly states the first two parts of an argument, as we diagram it below:

Grounds	Claim
Saddam Hussein has WMDs	*Saddam Hussein is a threat to the United States*

The third part of an argument in the Toulmin model identifies the reasoning implied by the grounds and the claim. This is the **warrant** in the argument. In our example above, what unstated premise must you accept in order to accept the claim?

Grounds	Warrant	Claim
Saddam Hussein has WMDs	*Saddam Hussein is likely to use WMDs against the United States*	*Saddam Hussein is a threat to the United States*

As you can see, without the warrant, we don't have the reasoning in the argument, which tells us why WMDs in the hands of Saddam Hussein are a threat to the United States. The warrant supplies the missing link in our argument. But the warrant itself needs support because it may be subject to dispute. And the probable truth of the claim may also hinge on the strength of an opposing argument. The Toulmin model considers this analysis by adding three more parts to the argument: the **reservation** (also called the ***rebuttal***) represents a likely counterpoint to the argument (e.g., having WMDs may not be a threat without an effective delivery system), the **backing** provides support for the warrant (e.g., citing research on the motives of Hussein), and the **qualifier** indicates how certain we are that the claim is true. The diagram below places these three elements into the argument above:

Grounds	Qualifier	Claim
Saddam Hussein has WMDs	*Probably*	*Saddam Hussein is a threat to the United States*
	Warrant	
	Saddam Hussein is likely to use WMDs against the United States	**Reservation**
	Backing	*Unless the Iraqis have no delivery system for the WMDs*
	Intelligence reports indicate that Saddam Hussein wants to attack the United States	

Independent and Interdependent Arguments

The simplest arguments contain a claim, a premise supporting the claim (grounds), and a premise supplying the reasoning in the argument (warrant). But this analysis ignores the fact that most claims do not depend on a single supporting premise (i.e., the grounds). For example, in support of the claim that *dogs make great pets*, we might argue that *they are dependable, affectionate, and intelligent.* In this argument, we have three **independent premises**—we assume that each premise offers a sufficient reason for accepting the claim that dogs make great pets: they are dependable, OR they are affectionate, OR they are intelligent.

In contrast, some arguments contain **interdependent premises**—none supports the claim sufficiently without the others. For example, suppose you claim that *Professor Jones should adopt a new textbook for her Argumentation and Debate course* because *(1) the textbook she requires now is difficult to read and (2) other available textbooks are easier to read.* Does each premise offer sufficient grounds for the claim? No. Why should she adopt a new textbook if the one she's using is not difficult to read? And why should she adopt a new textbook if other available textbooks are no less difficult? Together, the premises may offer sufficient grounds for the claim, but each premise standing alone does not.

Some arguments contain interdependent premises because each premise represents a link in a chain of events leading to a supposed result. These cause-effect arguments are only as strong as the weakest link in the chain. For example, take the following argument:

> *Violence on TV leads to violence in real life. Research shows that watching a lot of TV distorts our view of how violent the world is. This creates a kind of paranoia that makes people go out and buy guns for protection. And the more guns out there, the more potential there is for violence.*

This argument begins with the claim that *violence on TV leads to violence in real life.* How many premises does the argument contain as grounds for the claim? The answer is three. And notice how each premise is part of a series leading to the next premise and finally to the claim. Clearly, none of the premises alone provides sufficient support for the claim.

RECOGNIZING AND TESTING ARGUMENTS

In the opening of this chapter, we referred to the ongoing debate, taking place in communities across the United States, on the issue of smoking bans. Advocates of smoking bans point to the health and environmental risks of secondhand smoke, the ineffectiveness of nonsmoking areas and ventilation systems, and the public support for smoking bans; opponents question the dangers of secondhand smoke, prefer freedom of choice over government intrusion, and point to the economic impact on restaurants and bars. But how compelling are the arguments on both sides and how do we choose among competing claims? To be sure, questions of policy often come down to legitimate differences in values (e.g., health and safety vs. freedom of choice), and we will discuss this matter in Chapter 7. But determining the relative truth of a claim that requires critical thinking involves assessing the strength of evidence and reasoning. In the next chapter, we discuss types and tests of evidence; here we focus on that part of an inductive argument we too often take for granted—the reasoning. Below, we identify the most common types of reasoning along with the questions we should ask about how well the reasoning supports the claim (i.e., types and tests of reasoning).

Reasoning by Authority

Reasoning by authority bases the truth of a claim on the credibility of an external source. A speaker might argue, for example, that secondhand smoke is dangerous because the Surgeon General says it's dangerous. The reasoning asserts that the source, the Surgeon General, is both competent and trustworthy. Consider a second example, using the Toulmin model:

Grounds	Warrant	Claim
In a recent editorial, The Philadelphia Inquirer endorsed a smoking ban	*The Philadelphia Inquirer is a credible authority on the issue of smoking bans*	*Smoking should be banned in bars and restaurants*

In this argument, the claim that smoking should be banned in bars and restaurants depends directly on the grounds that the newspaper, the *Philadelphia Inquirer*, favors such bans. The warrant or reasoning in the argument tells us why the grounds are sufficient: the newspaper is a competent and trustworthy source of information on the topic of a smoking ban.

The test for this type of reasoning asks whether the source is, in fact, sufficiently credible to make the claim. Uncritical listeners too often accept the word of a so-called authority at face value. But there are two key questions all of us should raise.

First, is the source a legitimate authority on the subject? For instance, while we expect the *Philadelphia Inquirer*, like any newspaper, to express an opinion, the opinion doesn't necessarily carry greater authority than that of any informed citizen. Particularly on matters of fact (e.g., the effects of secondhand smoke), we should always try to distinguish between a primary source and a secondary source. Getting information from a ***primary source*** means getting it "from the horse's mouth," so to speak; from the person/s who actually observed the phenomena being reported (e.g., the author/s of a study, the witness to an event). Although ***secondary sources*** may differ in their credentials and level of expertise, the report of a primary source is much less likely to be misconstrued or distorted.

Second, does the source have any bias on the subject? Critics of the *Philadelphia Inquirer* frequently accuse the newspaper of exhibiting a "liberal slant" in its reporting and in its editorials. Such charges may or may not be true. But the existence of such a bias would be sufficient grounds for questioning the source. For instance, on the topic of smoking bans, we would expect a liberal advocate to endorse government intervention more readily (favor a smoking ban) and a more conservative or libertarian advocate to more eagerly choose the free market (oppose a smoking ban).

Reasoning by Definition

Reasoning by definition bases the truth of a claim on the essential features or nature of something. Implicit in this type of reasoning is some criteria on which to draw an interpretation or render a judgment. For example, opponents of smoking bans argue that patrons choose to visit bars and restaurants that permit smoking and are free to go elsewhere if they want a smoke-free environment; so we shouldn't think of nonsmokers as "innocent victims" under these circumstances. We can diagram this argument as follows:

Grounds	Warrant	Claim
Patrons choose the bars and restaurants they go to, and can go elsewhere	*Persons who inflict harm on themselves are not innocent victims*	*Patrons in public places where smoking is allowed are not innocent victims*

The test of this reasoning asks whether the definition and/or criteria contained in the argument is appropriate, and whether there are better, more useful, and perhaps less biased definitions and/or criteria. For instance, the argument above implies that we shouldn't be concerned with "protecting" people from themselves—people who are not innocent victims. The reasoning offers a definition of innocent victims as persons who do not inflict harm on themselves. Of course, by this definition, no adult in a bar or restaurant qualifies as an innocent victim because he or she "chose" to be there. But what about people who work in these establishments because they need the money? What about people who do not fully appreciate the health risks associated with passive smoking? Should we not care about their safety? Perhaps a less prejudicial definition of "innocent victims" should include persons who do not intend to hurt themselves.

Reasoning by Generalization

Reasoning by generalization bases the truth of a claim on one or more typical cases, arguing that what is true of some must be true of most. In the argument below, a speaker cites the results of a survey in Missouri to support the claim that most people support a smoking ban.[3]

Grounds	Warrant	Claim
A Missouri survey shows that a majority of the public support a smoking ban	People in Missouri are typical of most Americans	The public favors a ban on smoking in bars and restaurants

The test for this type of reasoning asks whether we can generalize from the cases provided in the grounds of the argument: Are there a sufficient number of cases and are they representative of all or most cases? All surveys, as in the one noted above, rely on this type of reasoning. Scientific surveys use random sampling methods that allow researchers to generalize from what may seem to be a small sample to a large population (e.g., predicting the outcome of a national election based on a sample of 1,500 likely voters).[4] In our argument above, while it may be possible to generalize about people living in Missouri (assuming this was a scientific survey), we cannot generalize about Americans; as a result, the reasoning in this argument is seriously flawed.

The results of surveys and polls rely on reasoning by generalization.

Reasoning by Analogy

Reasoning by analogy bases the truth of a claim on a comparison between two things, asserting that what is true of one is most likely true of the other. Implicit in this type of reasoning is the assumption that the similarities between the two things are more telling than are the differences. For instance, an opponent of smoking bans might say that people will violate a law telling them not to smoke in bars just as often as they now violate a law telling them not to speed on the highways. Another example, diagrammed below, assumes a similarity between bars and casinos:

Grounds	Warrant	Claim
Bars have lost a lot of business as a result of smoking bans	Smoking is as necessary for business in casinos as it is in bars	Casinos will lose a lot of business if we ban smoking

The test for reasoning by analogy asks whether the differences between the two things being compared invalidate the comparison. In other words, what's true of one thing may not be true of the other. Think about the two arguments above. The reasoning in the first assumes that rates of noncompliance with a smoking ban will be similar to those of a speeding limit. But are the two sufficiently similar? You could argue that violating a smoking ban is not as easy as violating a speeding limit. In the second argument, comparing casinos and bars, you could challenge the reasoning by arguing that it's easier for people to drink somewhere other than a bar than it is for people to gamble somewhere other than a casino. So casinos may not lose as much business as bars do because smoking may not be as necessary for business in casinos.

Reasoning by Cause

Reasoning by cause bases the truth of a claim on a cause-effect relationship between two things, one leading to the other. In this type of argument, the claim identifies the effect (consequent) and the grounds (premise) implicate the cause (antecedent). Let's suppose an opponent of smoking bans argues that a smoking ban in New York City led to increased unemployment in New York City bars and restaurants.

Grounds	Warrant	Claim
New York City bans smoking in bars and restaurants	*New York City's smoking ban causes increased layoffs in bars and restaurants*	*Layoffs in New York City bars and restaurants will continue to worsen*

The test for this type of reasoning directly challenges the cause-effect relationship alleged in the warrant. In this case, does a ban on smoking actually cause unemployment in bars and restaurants? If unemployment is in fact increasing, as stated in the claim, perhaps other factors related to a slowing economy are more to blame. Without sufficient backing from scientifically controlled studies showing a strong association between the ban and the subsequent layoffs, the reasoning in the argument is subject to considerable dispute (see *Post-Hoc Fallacy* in Chapter 4).

Reasoning by Sign

Reasoning by sign bases the truth of a claim on a relationship between two things where one indicates the other. In this type of argument, the indicator (or sign) appears in the grounds (premise), while the thing indicated by the sign appears in the claim. Although we generally hesitate to assume a causal relationship between the sign and what it indicates, this type of reasoning closely resembles *effect-to-cause reasoning* (i.e., the reverse of reasoning by cause). For instance, advocates of smoking bans frequently cite statistics showing decreased smoking in bars and restaurants where smoking is banned, as a clear sign that bans work. A more challenging argument, also using sign reasoning, claims that fewer smokers in bars and restaurants indicate not just compliance with the law, but also that smokers are quitting.

Grounds	Warrant	Claim
There is less smoking in bars and restaurants after smoking bans	*Less smoking after a ban indicates that bans encourage smokers to quit*	*Smokers are quitting in response to smoking bans*

The test for this type of reasoning questions whether a sign necessarily indicates one thing in particular more than another. In everyday life, signs can refer to many different things. A sneeze can indicate an allergy, a cold, or a tickle. As we all know, heavy traffic can indicate an accident, road construction, poor weather, rush hour, or a big event nearby. The same kind of critical thinking applies to policy debates. In the example above, assuming that the grounds are factually correct, and there is less smoking after a smoking ban (not surprising), does that necessarily indicate that smokers are quitting? More likely, smokers are staying away or just not smoking where it's banned. Certainly, we should not accept the reasoning in this argument at face value.

SUMMARY

Analyzing an argument, a vital critical thinking skill, means breaking an argument apart and studying the parts. All arguments contain a claim and a premise that supports the claim. The reasoning, often the unstated premise in an argument, shows how the premise supports the claim. One important distinction is between deductive and inductive arguments. Whereas deductive arguments are either valid or invalid, inductive arguments involve some degree of truth. The Toulmin model examines arguments by identifying the claim, grounds, warrant, backing, reservation, and qualifier. We also discussed the difference between arguments containing independent premises and those containing interdependent premises. Finally, we introduced six different types of arguments based on differences in reasoning and identified the tests associated with each: authority, definition, generalization, analogy, cause, and sign.

NOTES

1 On smoking, you've come a long way, Philly. (2012, November 27). *Philadelphia Inquirer,* A14. Retrieved from Newsbank Web.
2 Toulmin, S. (1976). *Knowing and acting.* New York, NY: Macmillan.
3 Schlinkmann, M. (2010, September 15). *Survey shows St. Charles County supports indoor smoking ban.* St. Louis Post-Dispatch, MO: Newspaper Source. Retrieved from EBSCOhost website: http://navigator-wcupa.passhe.edu/login?url=http://search.ebscohost.com/login.aspx?direct=true&db=nfh&AN=2W68486 57108&site=ehost-live&scope=site.
4 Frey, L., Botan, C., & Kreps, G. (2005). *Investigating communication: An introduction to research methods.* Boston, MA: Allyn & Bacon.

Chapter 3

Recognizing Fallacious Arguments

CHAPTER OUTLINE

I. Formal Fallacies

II. Informal Fallacies: Faulty Assumptions
   A. Arguing in a Circle
   B. Ignoring the Middle Ground
   C. Equating the Whole and the Parts
   D. Presuming Cause and Effect

III. Informal Fallacies: Diversionary Tactics
   A. Shifting the Burden of Proof
   B. Introducing an Irrelevant Point
   C. Attacking a Defenseless Argument
   D. Attacking the Person
   E. Appealing to Popular Prejudice

IV. Summary

KEY TERMS

Ad Hominem
Ad Populum
Appeal to ignorance
Begging the Question
The Fallacy of Composition
The Fallacy of Division
Fallacy
False Dilemma

Formal Fallacy
Informal Fallacy
Non sequitur
Post Hoc Fallacy
Red Herring
Slippery Slope
Straw Man Fallacy

Over a decade has passed since Oregon enacted the Death with Dignity Act, giving terminally ill individuals the legal right to end their lives through the voluntary self-administration of lethal medications prescribed by a physician for that purpose. The Oregon Act states that ending one's life in accordance with the law does not constitute suicide or assisted suicide, and it specifically prohibits lethal injection, mercy killing, or active euthanasia, where a physician or other person directly administers a medication to end another's life.[1]

Opponents of policies that hasten a movement toward physician-assisted suicide frequently point to the moral and ethical consequences of such policies, a position that resonates with large numbers of people. But occasionally, the position goes too far, as in the claim that any form of physician-assisted suicide will inevitably lead to mercy killing and a disregard for human life: "Before long," some people claim, "we'll be killing everyone afflicted with a terminal disease." This argument is an example of a **fallacy** (see the *slippery slope* fallacy below), a defective argument based on an error in reasoning and/or an attempt to mislead.

There are two broad classes of fallacies originating from the distinction between deductive and inductive arguments we discussed in the previous chapter. A flawed *deductive* argument is a **formal fallacy,** which involves an error in the structure of the argument, and a flawed *inductive* argument is an **informal fallacy,** which involves an array of faulty assumptions and questionable tactics that damage the process of argumentation. What all fallacies have in common is that on the surface the arguments may appear logical. But in fact they are not.

FORMAL FALLACIES

In our discussion of deductive arguments in Chapter 2, we noted that the claims in these arguments are either valid or invalid. That is, either we must accept the claim if we accept the premises (valid argument), or <u>we need not accept the claim if we accept the premises—the claim "does not follow" from the premises (invalid argument)</u>. A **non sequitur** is any argument containing a claim that does not follow from the premises. Thus, all invalid arguments are non sequiturs.

For instance, in Chapter 2 we presented the <u>valid</u> form of a categorical syllogism, where we must accept the claim if we accept the premises:

Major premise:	*All A's are B*	*All artists are creative*
Minor premise:	*C is A*	*Ted is an artist*
Claim:	*C is B*	*Ted is creative*

In contrast, consider the following invalid form:

Major premise:	*All A's are B*	*All artists are creative*
Minor premise:	*C is B*	*Ted is creative*
Claim:	*C is A*	*Ted is an artist*

This argument is invalid because none of the premises say that all creative people are artists. The fact that Ted is creative does not necessarily mean he's an artist (this is known as the fallacy of the *undistributed middle term*).

In Chapter 2, we also presented <u>valid</u> deductive arguments in the form of hypothetical syllogisms. For example, you may recall the following:

Affirming the Antecedent

Major premise:	*If A, then B*	*If it rains, the roof will leak*
Minor premise:	*A*	*It is raining*
Claim:	*B*	*The roof will leak*

Denying the Consequent

Major premise:	*If A, then B*	*If it rains, the roof will leak*
Minor premise:	*not B*	*The roof is not leaking*
Claim:	*not A*	*It did not rain*

While the above arguments are valid, the following forms below are <u>invalid</u>, though they may not seem to be at first sight:

Denying the Antecedent

Major premise:	*If A, then B*	*If it rains, the roof will leak*
Minor premise:	*not A*	*It is not raining*
Claim:	*not B*	*The roof will not leak*

Affirming the Consequent

Major premise:	*If A, then B*	*If it rains, the roof will leak*
Minor premise:	*B*	*The roof is leaking*
Claim:	*A*	*It rained*

These two invalid arguments contain claims that we need not accept. Both assume that the roof will only leak if it rains, but neither argument rules out the possibility that something other than rain can cause the roof to leak (e.g., washing the roof, lawn sprinklers hitting the roof, melting snow on the roof, etc.).

All formal fallacies involve errors in the structure of an argument, leading to claims that need not follow from the premises. In the next two sections, we consider a number of informal fallacies: common mistakes based on misguided assumptions and/or diversionary tactics.

INFORMAL FALLACIES: FAULTY ASSUMPTIONS

Each of these informal fallacies is based on a faulty assumption. In one way or another, the reasoning in these arguments fails to support the claim. Therefore, we can regard all of them as *non sequiturs.*

Arguing in a Circle

One of the most irksome and difficult to recognize fallacies is **begging the question,** a fallacy based on the false assumption that a given premise supports a claim when in fact there is little substantive difference between the premise and the claim. Like all fallacies, its resemblance to a sound argument belies the fact that it is not. Take a look at the following:

- *"There is no doubt that God exists because the Bible says so."*
- *"Capital punishment is immoral because it's wrong to kill someone."*
- *"We are not succeeding in Iraq because we haven't completed the mission."*

In each of the above "arguments," a close look reveals little difference between the claim and the premise. So, when we challenge the premise, the speaker may simply restate the claim (or some version of the claim) as support for the premise, which is why another name for this fallacy is *circular reasoning.*

Speaker:	"There is no doubt that God exists. The Bible says so."
Challenge:	"Why should we believe the Bible?"
Speaker:	"Because the Bible is the word of God."

Speaker: "Capital punishment is immoral. It's wrong to kill someone."
Challenge: "Why is it wrong?"
Speaker: "Because killing people is immoral."

Speaker: "We are not succeeding in Iraq. We haven't completed the mission."
Challenge: "How do you know we haven't completed the mission?"
Speaker: "Because we have not been successful."

Ignoring the Middle Ground

One of the most common fallacies, and also one of the most recognizable, is the **false dilemma** (or false dichotomy). Sometimes called the "either or" fallacy, this defective argument occurs when the reasoning in an argument assumes the existence of only two alternatives, when in fact there are more than two. In other words, they assume mistakenly that things are "black or white." Of course, more often than not, the "gray" area is a viable option. Consider the following examples:

- An opponent of pulling troops out of Iraq argues: *"If you're not supporting the war on terror you're supporting the terrorists."*
- An advocate of physician-assisted suicide says: *"Do you want to relieve the pain and suffering of terminally ill patients or not? By refusing to support this plan, you are forcing them to endure a life of misery and despair."*

In the first example, is there a middle ground between supporting the war and supporting the terrorists? If not, then everyone who opposes the war is supporting the terrorists, which is certainly not the case, particularly among critics who advocate different ways of fighting the terrorists. This kind of polarizing rhetoric, "either you're for us or against us," sets up a false dilemma that, in the end, appeals more to our emotions than to our capacity for critical thinking. Similarly, in the second example, the advocate of physician-assisted suicide overlooks the myriad ways we now try to help terminally ill patients live out the remainder of their lives with dignity and in comfort (e.g., hospice care). This false dilemma assumes wrongly that physician-assisted suicide is the only alternative to pain and suffering now available to terminally ill patients.

Of course, we should never dismiss an argument just because it poses a dilemma. Sometimes there is no "middle ground" and a dilemma is not false. For instance, in the ongoing debate over Roe v. Wade, there is nothing fallacious in the claim that you can't be prochoice and at the same time be in favor of an absolute ban on all abortions. On the other hand, since you can be prochoice and against abortions, it would be a false dilemma to claim that one must choose between these two positions.

Equating the Whole and the Parts

On July 8, 2010, LeBron James announced his decision to take his "talents" to South Beach to play for the Miami Heat. With the addition of James to the team, the assumption was that Miami was a great team and would win the NBA Championship in 2010–11. But the argument that the team would be great because each of the players on the team is great, illustrates the **fallacy of composition**, assuming that what is true of the parts must be true of the whole. This was true for Miami during the 2010–11 season as the Heat did not win the NBA Championship.

The converse, known as the **fallacy of division**, assumes that what is true of the whole must be true of the parts. This can be applied to the Miami Heat during the next two NBA seasons as Miami won the NBA Championship, not because each of their players was a superstar, but because each person learned how to play together as a team. Just because the team won the championship doesn't mean all 12 players on the roster are superstars. Because these two fallacies are so similar, it's easy to mistake one for the other. In each of the examples listed below, can you tell which ones are fallacies of composition and which ones are fallacies of division?

- *"That house must be 50 years old, so I suppose everything inside is probably falling apart and needs to be replaced."*
- *"All of the programs on that network must be top-rated since that network has the highest rating."*
- *"Sharon is a fun person to be around and Mark is a fun person to be around. Having them both over for dinner should be a lot of fun."*
- *"I don't understand why you don't want to buy that new chocolate pizza at the store. You love chocolate and you love pizza, don't you?"*

In the examples above, if you said the first two are fallacies of division and the second two are fallacies of composition, you are correct. The first two assume that what is true of the whole (the house, the network) must be true of the parts (everything inside the house; each of the programs); the second two assume that what is true of the parts (fun persons; chocolate and pizza) must be true of the whole (the couple; chocolate pizza).

At first glance, the fallacy of composition may resemble an unwarranted generalization, in which you assume, based on too few cases, that what is true of some cases (a sample) is true of most or all cases (a population). For instance, someone might claim that all the players on a team are great because some players on that team are great. But the fallacy of composition equates all the players on the team, with the team (parts/whole), not some players, with all the players (sample/population).

Presuming Cause and Effect

Steven's parents enroll him in a martial arts class. Two months later, Steven gets in a fight at school with one of his classmates. His parents begin to worry that the martial arts class might be to blame. "Maybe the lessons are making him more aggressive," his dad says. Of course, while the martial arts class could be partly responsible, it is just as likely, given the lack of any evidence, that something else entirely caused the fight between Steven and his classmate. The claim that one event (A) causes another event (B), simply because (A) precedes (B) illustrates the **post hoc fallacy.**

Since one of the requirements of a cause-effect relationship is that the cause precedes the effect, it's only natural that we would look backward in time when trying to locate the cause of an event (e.g., trying to figure out what caused your headache or your heartburn). But doing so without the benefit of a controlled study that attempts to "rule out" other causes is problematic.

The post hoc fallacy often appears in arguments over the effectiveness of public policy. Take the example of gun control. In an article entitled, "The Media Campaign Against Gun Ownership," columnist Phyllis Schlafly wrote:

The only policy that effectively reduces public shootings is right-to-carry laws. Allowing citizens to carry concealed handguns reduces violent crime. In the 31 states that have passed right-to-carry laws since the mid-1980s, the number of multiple-victim public shootings and other violent crimes has dropped dramatically. Murders fell by 7.65%, rapes by 5.2%, aggravated assaults by 7%, and robberies by 3%.[2]

In the absence of any research "ruling out" other likely causes of reduced crime in these states (e.g., increased spending on law enforcement), or comparing crime rates among these states and those without right-to-carry laws, the simple claim that right-to-carry laws caused a reduction in violent crime is a post hoc fallacy.

Another well-known fallacy presuming cause and effect is the **slippery slope.** You may recall that we began this chapter with an illustration of this fallacy—the claim that if we legalized physician-assisted suicide, it wouldn't be long before we started killing off everyone with a terminal disease. The defining feature of all slippery slope fallacies is the assumption that one event will trigger an unavoidable series of events that eventually produce a horrific result. Here are a few examples:

- *"Colleges and universities keep increasing tuition. Pretty soon only the rich will be able to afford a higher education, and everyone else will have to settle for a high school diploma"*
- *"Some say we should legalize the use of marijuana for medicinal purposes. But if we do that, the next thing you know, we'll be legalizing pot and cocaine for everyone."*
- *"We shouldn't support stem cell research without considering the long-term consequences. Do we really want to live in a society where we end up with human cloning and "designer" children?"*

The difference between a legitimate *chain argument,* where each link in a chain of events leads to the next (see Chapter 2) and a slippery slope fallacy is that the chain argument identifies and provides support for each link in the chain, while the slippery slope fallacy does not. Of course, this doesn't mean that slippery slopes never come true. Back when restaurants began providing nonsmoking sections, there were no doubt plenty of slippery slope arguments predicting a ban on smoking in all public places, an outcome that may have seemed horrific at that time.

Despite the flawed logic, people often use slippery slope arguments for dramatic effect, as a rhetorical device, a "call to arms" among concerned citizens. Moreover, a slippery slope that may strike us as overly dramatic at first may seem more reasonable with the benefit of historical hindsight. One of the most memorable examples of this occurs in the classic 1960 film, *Inherit the Wind,* about the well-known "Scopes Monkey Trial" of 1925. Actor Spencer Tracy, depicting the great trial attorney Clarence Darrow defending a teacher accused of violating a law against teaching evolution to his students warns of the perils of such a law:

"If today you can take a thing like evolution and make it a crime to teach it in the public school, tomorrow you can make it a crime to teach it in the private schools. At the next session you may ban books and the newspapers. Soon you may set Catholic against Protestant and Protestant against Protestant, and try to foist your own religion upon the minds of men. If you can do one you can do the other. Ignorance and fanaticism is ever busy and needs feeding. Always it is feeding and gloating for more. . . . After a while, your honor, it is the setting of man against man and creed against creed until with flying banners and beating drums we are marching backward to the glorious ages of the sixteenth century when bigots [burned] the men who dared to bring any intelligence and enlightenment and culture to the human mind."[3]

The post hoc and slippery slope fallacies are not the only flaws in reasoning from cause to effect. Another common error occurs when we mistake *correlation* for causation. To illustrate, let's consider the research on factors contributing to childhood obesity. One factor under considerable scrutiny is the media. Do television, video games, and the Internet cause childhood obesity? In fact, studies show that kids who sit in front of a screen for hours on end are more likely to be overweight than kids who don't.[4] But do these studies alone prove that the media causes obesity? The answer is no, because correlation is not the same thing as causation.

One reason for being cautious about inferring causality from correlation is the possibility of *ignoring a common cause.* That is, a third factor might be responsible for a correlation between the presumed cause and effect. For instance, maybe kids are more likely to overeat and watch TV if they are mildly depressed or if they have a certain personality type. Another reason for being cautious when inferring causality from correlation is the "chicken-or-the-egg" problem: which came first? Does watching TV cause kids to become obese or does obesity cause kids to watch TV? For these reasons, most researchers design controlled experiments that "rule out" the influence of other factors while also establishing which factor is the cause and which is the effect.[5]

INFORMAL FALLACIES: DIVERSIONARY TACTICS

Up to this point, we have discussed fallacies based on various flaws in the reasoning of an argument. Now we consider a number of fallacies used as diversionary tactics, whether deliberate or not. What these fallacies have in common is that they often refer to an opposing argument and they draw our attention away from the logic of an argument.

Shifting the Burden of Proof

As we pointed out in Chapter 2, a claim without any supporting evidence—a groundless claim—is not an argument but a mere assertion. In a dispute between opposing claims, such as a debate, we expect one side or the other to offer convincing proof of a claim. We call this the *burden of proof* (see Chapter 5). Trying to support a claim by pointing to the lack of evidence against that claim is usually an **appeal to ignorance,** a fallacy that attempts to escape the burden of proof by giving it to one's adversary. Here are two rather obvious examples:

> *Alyssa:* "I believe there is life on other planets."
> *Carla:* "That's pretty unlikely."
> *Alyssa:* "Well, no one has been able to prove there isn't"

> *Greg:* "The Flyers will win the Stanley Cup this year"
> *Howard:* "Are you kidding? There's no way."
> *Greg:* "Why won't they?"

In both examples, the first speakers, Alyssa and Greg, make rather bold claims that require some evidence and reasoning to be convincing, but neither speaker offers any proof, choosing instead to shift that burden to the speaker who disagrees with them.

While the above examples are clearly fallacious, sometimes a sound argument may resemble an appeal to ignorance even though it is not. Consider the following:

> *Paula:* "Taking vitamins to prevent the flu doesn't work."
> *Mike:* "You're wrong. Taking vitamins is a great idea."
> *Paula:* "No one has been able to prove that vitamins work."

Is Paula shifting the burden of proof to Mike? Is she appealing to ignorance in an effort to avoid proving her claim? Our answer is it depends on two factors. First, does the speaker make a claim that challenges existing beliefs and policies? If so, that speaker needs a convincing argument, one that requires proof. Arguing that life exists on other planets, or that the Flyers will win the Stanley Cup (which has not happened since the 1970s), are claims that clearly challenge existing beliefs. However, Paula's claim that taking vitamins doesn't prevent the flu coincides with current beliefs (see Chapter 5 for more on this point). Second, when Paula asserts that no one has been able to prove vitamins prevent the flu, she may be referring to studies that failed to find a link between vitamins and the flu, in which case she is referring to evidence that actually supports her claim.

Introducing an Irrelevant Point

Perhaps the most blatant yet surprisingly successful diversionary tactic is bringing up an irrelevant claim instead of responding to an opposing claim. The tactic works when an opposing speaker takes the bait and abandons the original point of contention. The irrelevant claim is called a **red herring,** a name that originates from the British sport of fox hunting, in which a smoked herring, red in color, is dragged across the trail of a fox to throw the hounds off the scent, giving the fox an opportunity to escape.[6] Likewise, the red herring fallacy provides an opportunity for a speaker to "escape" an opposing argument. For example, in a dispute over whether violence on television has harmful consequences, the claim that parents aren't doing enough to monitor what their children watch, is a red herring. While the claim is relevant in a policy dispute over what should be done about television violence, it isn't relevant in a dispute over whether television violence is harmful. Similarly, in a policy dispute over what should be done about the problem of global warming, the claim that we should worry less about global warming and more about global terrorism is a red herring unless the two policies are mutually exclusive (i.e., we can't fight global warming and global terrorism, so we must choose one or the other).

Attacking a Defenseless Argument

A fairly common though fallacious practice in argumentation is attributing a baseless claim to the opposing side and then "proving" that the claim is baseless. In this practice, the guilty party disproves a claim the other side never made in the first place. The name of this fallacy is the **straw man**, derived from the practice of using straw men resembling the enemy for targets in combat training.[7] Thus, in this fallacy, a speaker attacks a "straw man" or defenseless argument instead of a worthy argument. Although the straw man fallacy is a mainstay in the rhetoric of campaign politics, *Washington Post* columnist Dana Milbank cited a historical example from then President Bush as one of the more prolific practitioners.[8] In his article, "Making Hay out of Straw Men," Milbank describes a number of instances. For example, in one particular speech addressing, the importance of integrity in government, business, and the military, the President challenged people who practice "moral relativism" to defend their belief that everyone is equally right on every moral issue.

Attacking the Person

The straw man fallacy is not the only diversionary tactic favored in the "rough-and-tumble" world of partisan politics. Stump speeches and negative campaign ads are filled with **ad hominem** arguments, attacking an opponent's character instead of the opponent's stand on an issue. In general, questions of character are relevant in political campaigns, but they are not relevant when arguing a proposition unrelated to personal character. For instance, it's fair to criticize a political rival for being dishonest or inexperienced when claiming that he or she lacks the qualifications for office. But it would be fallacious and unfair to introduce these character issues when arguing about the merits of a health-care program for senior citizens.

In one particular form of ad hominem, a speaker argues that his or her opponent is a hypocrite. That is, the speaker claims that we should reject the opponent's argument because the argument condemns something the opponent is guilty of doing. For example, we shouldn't believe a speaker's claim that cocaine is dangerous because she used cocaine in college; or we must reject a speaker's claim that marital infidelity is wrong because he cheated on his wife. In neither case, is the action of the speaker—hypocritical though it may be—grounds for dismissing the speaker's evidence and reasoning.

Appealing to Popular Prejudice

Just because a belief is popular doesn't mean the belief is true. Not many years ago, most people believed all fatty foods were unhealthy, but now we talk about "good" fat and "bad" fat. Most people used to believe that cigarette smoking was little more than a bad habit, but now we know differently. Likewise, policies that were once taken for granted, such as those condoning sexual harassment or racial profiling, are now widely unpopular and actively discouraged.

The fallacy, **ad populum**, does not lie in the claim that most people have certain beliefs, but in the claim that something is true or good merely because most people believe it to be true or good (also called the ***bandwagon fallacy***). For example, if you assert that illegal immigration hurts more than it helps the economy, the results of a poll may tell us whether most people share this belief but not whether it is true. Similarly, the results of a poll suggesting that most Americans favor stem cell research does not tell us whether stem cell research will do more good than harm.

SUMMARY

This chapter examined the important critical thinking task of recognizing fallacious arguments–defective arguments based on an error in reasoning and/or an attempt to mislead. A flawed *deductive* argument is a formal fallacy, which involves an error in the structure of the argument, and a flawed *inductive* argument is an informal fallacy, which involves various faulty assumptions and questionable tactics that damage the process of argumentation. All fallacies may appear reasonable on the surface, but they are not.

Informal fallacies include faulty assumptions that ignore the middle ground, argue in a circle, equate the whole and the parts, and presume cause and effect. These fallacies also include a variety of diversionary tactics such as shifting the burden of proof, introducing an irrelevant point, attacking a defenseless argument, attacking the person instead of the argument, and appealing to popular prejudice.

NOTES

1 *Death with Dignity Act.* Retrieved from http://www.oregon.gov/DHS/ph/pas/about_us.shtml.

2 Schlafly, P. (2000, June). The media campaign against gun ownership. *The Phyllis Schlafly Report*, 33.

3 Excerpted from the movie, *Inherit the Wind* (1960).

4 *The role of media in childhood obesity.* (2004, February). Issue Brief, The Henry J. Kaiser Family Foundation, Washington, DC. Retrieved from http://www.kaisemetwork.org/health_cast/hcast_index.cfm?display=detail&hc=1087.

5 *Experimental design.* Retrieved from http://www.socialresearchmethods.net/kb/desexper.php.

6 *Definition of red herring fallacy.* Retrieved from http://www.fallacyfiles.org/redherrf.html.

7 *Definition of straw man fallacy.* Retrieved from http://en.wikipedia.org/wiki/Fallacy#General_list_of_fallacies.

8 Milbank, D. (2004, June 1). Making hay out of straw men. *The Washington Post*, p. A21.

Using and Testing Evidence

CHAPTER OUTLINE

KEY TERMS

Bias

Citing a Source

Completeness

Consistency

Corroboration

Credibility

Currency

Database

Examples

Evidence

Facts

Narratives

Primary Source

Secondary Source

Statistics

Testimony

Tertiary Source

We began our first chapter by referring to the Bush Administration's decision to invade Iraq as an example of argumentation. If we relate the Bush Administration's argumentation to Toulmin's model of argument, the claim would be that Saddam Hussein was an imminent threat to the United States, and the grounds would be that Hussein possessed weapons of mass destruction (WMDs). Claims, as this example illustrates, are easy to make; however, the challenge for any speaker is to provide proof to support the claim and thus make the argument stronger. As you know, for an argument to be successful, the speaker must provide the audience with "good reasons" to accept the proof that supports a claim.[1] In Toulmin's model, proof takes the form of evidence (the grounds) and reasoning (the warrant). In Chapters 2 and 3, we explained how we use reasoning to support an argument and what to avoid; and, in this chapter, we will focus on using and testing evidence to support our claims.

Evidence is external data that proves a point. Your evidence should come from an external source (such as book or newspaper) and it should be verified to be true. In the case of Iraq and the claim that it possessed WMDs, it was not until much later (after the invasion) that it was determined that the evidence the United States used as proof was not true.[2] Reviewers of government documents the Bush Administration used to justify the war discovered that some key information that was false was attributed to an Iraqi defector who turned out to have no credibility. This example illustrates the importance of testing and verifying evidence before using it to support a claim.

For this reason, we will identify and discuss how to use and test evidence. When speakers evaluate and verify the evidence they use for proof, it strengthens the arguments they present. Evidence must be scrutinized to determine its credibility and reliability. In this chapter, we will elaborate on the most common types of evidence, how to categorize evidence, and how to evaluate the evidence before using it to support an argument.

TYPES OF EVIDENCE

In the Toulmin model, evidence is used to support a claim. Speakers should carefully and ethically choose the best evidence to serve as proof for arguments. When using evidence, there are different types speakers can use, and each type has its strengths and weaknesses. The types of evidence we will discuss include facts, statistics, examples, opinions, and narratives.

Facts

Factual evidence is one of the most frequently used types of evidence. A **fact** is information we can verify to be true. In other words, a fact will always be the same regardless of its source. For example, it is a fact that the United States Constitution was officially ratified and became effective on March 4, 1789. This fact would be confirmed through various sources such as government documents, newspaper accounts, and historical documents. Although these sources are different, they report the same date when the U.S. Constitution was officially ratified. Checking different sources to determine whether the fact is true or not, illustrates one way speakers can verify evidence.

However, if the speaker stated that the U.S. Constitution having been in effect since 1789 makes the United States the best democracy, the statement (although based on a fact) would be an opinion. This example highlights how facts themselves, while referring to specific events, data, or occurrences, are open to interpretation if a speaker attempts to use a fact to support an opinion.

Statistics

Statistics are a second type of evidence that can support a claim. **Statistics** are numbers used to represent information. Commonly, statistics are used to indicate significance (how much), frequency (how often), correlation (how much

Statistics can bolster the claims and credibility of a speaker.

of a relationship), and effects (how much impact). Although statistics are widely used, unless the speaker or audience is familiar with how the statistic is calculated, how it is being used to represent information, and how it is being interpreted, it can be very misleading. For example, product statements that say four out of five doctors recommend a certain product, is a classic example of how statistics are misleading. Challenging this statement would lead to questions about the doctors referred to in the message, their expertise, and the relationship between the doctors and the product. Furthermore, the statistic may come from a sample that is too small to support the generalization.

For these reasons, speakers should always attempt to understand as much as possible how the statistic was determined, the source it was taken from, and the sample size of the study. When using statistics, it is wise to use a qualifier when stating the statistic such as, "According to the *Philadelphia Inquirer's* telephone poll of 5,000 registered voters, 60% favor the state of Pennsylvania legalizing casino gambling."

In addition, when using statistics, speakers should adhere to specific guidelines. First, speakers should verify that the statistic is directly related to the specific proposition. Suppose a speaker argued that theft has increased on college campuses by 10%. On the surface, the statistic seems significant. However, while the statistic does support the claim (that theft has increased), it does not relate to the claim because the source in which the statistic was acquired came from a report of crime on urban campuses. Since the evidence refers to urban campuses, it does not relate to the specific claim of crime on suburban campuses.

This is why speakers have to conduct research ethically and test it ahead of time to make sure it is appropriate. In order for the evidence to be relevant to the claim, a speaker needs to either gather statistics from a study that analyzes crime on suburban campuses (or a similar suburban campus) or obtain statistics from the campus' public safety department. In either of these instances, the evidence would be a more reliable form of proof because it is related to the particular claim.

Second, speakers need to make sure the statistic is typical of the trend and not the exception. A few years ago, the housing market was very hot as many "investors" were engaged in buying homes and "flipping" them to make a profit. Many other people decided to join the market due to record setting housing sales. Although some early investors saw their profits increase 150%, it did not mean that each investor who followed would make the same profit. In addition, there were many factors that contributed to the record sales such as interest rates, job market, location, housing demand, and new home construction. Instead of using a record statistic or a statistic from a hot housing market, the wise investor would need to investigate these factors and review the 10-year housing trend in the same location to ascertain the potential profit in house flipping.

Third, speakers should make the statistic as meaningful as possible. Sometimes, the numbers that are presented in an argument are too large for the audience to fully comprehend. For example, watchdog groups that monitor the national debt indicate that it is over $16 trillion. Sixteen trillion dollars is an immense amount of money and the enormity of the figure can be difficult to appreciate. However, if we simplify the statistic for the audience by explaining that $16 trillion roughly equates to each person in the United States (man, woman, and child) owing $189,000, the simplification of the statistic conveys the significance of the problem more effectively.

Examples

Examples, another type of evidence, are specific cases that support a claim. Examples can be thought of as illustrations of the claim. Used properly, examples enable a speaker to explain or clarify an idea or concept to the audience. In addition, examples can take an unfamiliar idea and make it more understandable though a familiar example. For instance, a speaker could use the example of an individual running up personal debt on a credit card to familiarize the audience with the way the national debt affects the government.

Examples can be actual and hypothetical. *Actual examples* are specific cases that occurred in real life. *Hypothetical examples* are not real, but should be based upon relevant and verifiable facts. When using either an actual or hypothetical example as proof, speakers need to be sure that the example is within the realm of possibility. If it is not, the audience will reject it regardless of whether it is actual or hypothetical.

To illustrate, consider an argument in which a speaker used the case of a Pennsylvania resident who won $1 million gambling on sports in Delaware (where it is legal) as proof that Pennsylvania should also legalize sports gambling. On the one hand, if the individual winning $1 million were an actual case, the audience would most likely reject the example (and the argument) because the audience would probably perceive the example as being very rare and thus unlikely to occur for most people. On the other hand, if the case were a hypothetical example, it would also be rejected because it is not within the realm of probability.

Not every example will serve as a form of proof, and some examples will work better with some audiences than with others.[3] Therefore, speakers need to make sure that the examples chosen to support a claim are logical and the relationship between example and claim is easily understood. Overall, examples are effective as a form of proof when the following occurs: 1) they clarify a process, occurrence, or event; 2) they illustrate a point; and 3) they are logically linked to the claim.

Testimony

A fourth type of evidence that speakers can use to support a claim is testimony. **Testimony** is an opinion that is expressed as a direct quotation. *Expert testimony* is opinion that comes from a person who is acknowledged as an authority or expert in a particular field. Meanwhile, *lay testimony* is opinion that comes from an ordinary person.

Both expert and lay testimony can be used as proof, most notably when it is providing description, explanation, and/or analysis. For example, consider a debate on immigration. If a speaker used a direct quotation from the Director of Homeland Security explaining the dangers people face in attempting to cross the U.S./Mexican border, the expert testimony would be used appropriately as proof. The expert testimony would be appropriate because the testimony is providing explanation and analysis. Likewise, using the direct quotation from a person who crossed the border would be an appropriate use of lay testimony because the testimony is providing a description and explanation of that person's experience of crossing the border.

Speakers, however, should avoid the temptation of using testimony alone to prove a claim. The statement from the person, whether an expert or not, is not sufficient to prove a claim. Testimony is very subjective, and when a speaker uses it to prove a claim, it is unclear if the person giving testimony was actually advocating the speaker's position or how the person reached his/her conclusion (i.e., personal experience, interpretation of a study, etc.).

Instead, testimony should be used primarily to describe, explain, or analyze an issue or situation. The power of testimony is not in attempting to prove a claim, but in authenticating, personalizing, and/or dramatizing the claim. Testimony can call attention to a problem, issue, or cause, while also establishing identification with the audience.

Narratives

Narratives are stories that have a logical point. Narratives may not be the strongest type of evidence because they are sometimes unverifiable, subjective, and emotional. However, as we mentioned in Chapter 1, different cultures have developed different rhetorical strategies that underlie their cultural beliefs and norms. For many cultures and cocultures, narratives represent cultural beliefs that influence individual ideas of what is right and wrong along with providing the motivation and reasoning for how to act and behave. The logical power of narratives lies in how stories tell truths about a culture's beliefs that organize reality while representing and explaining experience.[4]

Narratives underscore cultural beliefs that we discussed in Chapter 1. For example, American culture has many cultural beliefs such as "the possibility of success," the idea that if anyone works hard and plays by the rules, the person will achieve success.[5] Many stories of the underdog illustrate the possibility of success such as David and Goliath or Rocky, where the most unassuming and unlikely person through hard work and perseverance becomes the hero. Stories of the underdog also highlight our culture's value on individualism that underlines many of our public policies from immigration to abortion.

Typically, narratives are part of a culture's oral tradition where information, perspectives, values, and norms are passed down from generation to generation. The power of narratives lies not in whether the story is true but in the principle behind the story (sometimes they are both). For example, when Martin Luther King, Jr. gave his "I Have a Dream" speech, he used a narrative based upon the American value that "all men are created equal" to argue for the civil rights of African Americans.[6] Likewise, when Ronald Reagan gave a tribute to the Challenger astronauts who lost their lives when the Challenger exploded, he used a narrative that reiterated the American value of "conquering the frontier" and thus saved the U.S. space program.[7] Both examples illustrate the influence of narratives in shaping public debate.

Ultimately, narratives motivate the audience to act based upon deeply held cultural beliefs and values. Therefore, narratives are effective forms of proof when used to: 1) reinforce cultural beliefs and values that provide the reasoning for public policies and societal standards; 2) personalize issues or events; and 3) make issues or events more dramatic. Narratives, when used effectively, can connect cultural beliefs to individual emotions to influence how individuals accept or reject arguments.

Facts, statistics, examples, testimony, and narratives are different types of evidence that, when used carefully and ethically, can prove an argument. When speakers plan their presentations, they should attempt to use these different types of evidence strategically to support claims. Part of the strategic use of evidence is testing and evaluating the sources in which the evidence is acquired.

CATEGORIZING EVIDENCE

Now that we have identified and discussed the types of evidence and how speakers can use the different types of evidence effectively in a presentation, we can shift our attention to the sources in which evidence is gathered. Evaluating evidence begins by first classifying the possible sources in which evidence can be acquired. In general, the more reliable the source of the evidence, the stronger the argument the speaker can make. Sources can be categorized as primary, secondary, or tertiary. We will discuss each type next.

Primary Source

A **primary source** includes documents, physical objects, original works, or eyewitness accounts that were created during the actual historical time period that is being examined. When speakers have a primary source, they can observe the actual time period or event without the source being filtered through the interpretation of someone else.

Examples of primary evidence include but are not limited to:

- Speeches
- Diaries
- Letters
- Interviews (legal proceedings, personal, telephone, e-mail)
- Manuscripts
- News footage (video or audio recordings)
- Photographs
- Proceedings of meetings (conferences, symposiums)
- Survey research (market surveys, opinion polls)
- Original/legal documents (birth certificates, court records, tax records, property records, academic transcripts)
- Creative works (novels, essays, poetry, music, art)
- Broadcast transcripts

A great advantage of a primary source is that individuals can observe and evaluate the original document in its entirety and come to their own conclusions. For example, the evidence an individual gets from viewing a speech of the President is much more valuable than simply relying on newspaper articles of that speech. Newspaper articles will select specific parts of the President's speech, which influences the writing of the story and thus the evidence that can be gathered from it. Moreover, additional factors such as the type of newspaper and reporter bias will also impact the evidence presented in the article. Instead, if individuals viewed the actual speech of the President, they would be able to observe the speech in its entirety and make their own interpretation and evaluation of the speech.

Secondary Source

A **secondary source** is a document that was created after the actual time period that is being examined. A secondary source does not enable the researcher to observe the evidence in its entirety. Instead, secondary sources provide analysis, interpretation, and evaluation of a primary source. Moreover, individuals who create secondary sources tend to have no *personal* experience with the historical era or events.

The authors of secondary sources offer explanations and descriptions of primary sources, often quoting them within the text of the work. It is not uncommon for a secondary source to use primary sources as evidence to present a particular opinion or point of view.

Examples of secondary evidence include but are not limited to:

- Biographies
- Books
- Commentaries/Editorials
- Journal articles
- Newspaper articles
- Magazine articles

Sometimes, the line between a primary and secondary source is blurred, especially with news articles. However, if the source was recorded or commented on at the time it was happening, and the individual can observe the evidence in its entirety, the source is a primary source. For example, although a newspaper article might include eyewitness accounts that were written at the time of the event, it would still be considered a secondary source. The article would be labeled as a secondary source because an individual would not be able to observe the eyewitness testimony in its entirety. Furthermore, the author of the newspaper article selected which testimony to include, exclude, and edit in the article. However, if the newspaper article simply listed the full interview testimony (without editing it), then it would be considered a primary source.

Tertiary Source

The third category of sources is tertiary. A **tertiary source** is evidence that compiles, summarizes, reports, or lists information from other sources. A tertiary source exists if the primary purpose of the source is to list or summarize ideas that come from other sources.

Examples of tertiary sources follow:

- Abstracts
- Dictionaries and encyclopedias
- Directories
- Brochures and manuals

A **tertiary source** does not provide strong support for a claim for academic debate and research because the evidence from this source is not "raw material" and often comes from several sources that are often not identified. Moreover, these sources often provide little more than common knowledge on a topic and do not offer in-depth advanced research.

Understanding the different categories of sources can be compared to the strength of caffeine in coffee. Black, regular coffee will contain the maximum amount of caffeine because nothing has been mixed into the coffee to dilute its strength. Black coffee is like primary evidence; it is unfiltered and enables the individual to experience caffeine's maximum strength. Adding a teaspoon of cream to it causes the coffee to lose its maximum strength, but it still packs enough power to allow the individual to experience some of the caffeine's potency. This example is like secondary evidence as the individual experiences some strength of the caffeine. Finally, if a cup of regular coffee has the same amount of cream as it has coffee (a cupful), the strength of the caffeine of the coffee becomes very diluted and weak—much like tertiary evidence.

Web pages, while making information more accessible, should be scrutinized using the tests of evidence.

Web Pages

In our classification of the types of sources in which evidence is gathered, we did not list where web pages fit into the categorization (in referring to web pages we mean information that is found on the Internet, not information obtained from online research databases). Web pages, unlike the traditional primary, secondary, and tertiary sources, blur some distinctions while posing new issues such as credibility, bias, and reliability. For this reason, we include a specific section in the testing evidence section of this chapter on how to evaluate web pages to determine whether it is a credible source for supporting claims.

In short, web pages are considered "soft research" as the information is subjective and based on opinion. If conducting research on the web is to be considered, it should meet the tests of evidence we discuss later on in the chapter and it should focus on sites that offer more reliable information, such as academic journals, government agencies (such as the Center for Disease Control), government publications (such as the Congressional Budget Office), along with science and medical content not sanctioned by advertising or sponsorship (such as the New England Journal of Medicine).

In general, we are more cautious about recommending web pages as much as other sources because even official home pages of organizations are often biased, difficult to verify, and contain little more than tertiary sources. Using research databases to find primary and secondary sources will yield much better information than finding information from the web. In the next section, we discuss how to conduct "hard research" through online research databases.

ONLINE RESEARCH

The discussion of categorizing evidence by its sources leads to methods of conducting research to find good evidence. In general, there are no shortcuts to research. You need to plan in advance and use the best research available in order to construct a convincing argument. Good research takes time and effort, from locating the proper research engines, acquiring information from research databases, and reading/reviewing the information you find. Researchers often use an online research database in order to obtain evidence to support an argument. We discuss the use of these databases next.

There are no short cuts to research; it takes time, patience, and persistence.

Electronic Sources (Research Databases)

A **database** is an organized collection of information that can be accessed electronically. Library databases contain thousands of sources from popular news magazines to specialized journals that individuals can research in order to find information on a topic. Databases contain primary and secondary sources that are readily available for use. In addition, most databases contain a large portion of full-text articles, which makes information even more assessable.

Database providers like, *EBSCOhost,* and databases such as *National Newspapers Core, CQ Researcher,* and *LexisNexis* will generate primary and secondary sources you can review to find evidence. These and other types of databases for academic research can serve as a powerful tool for obtaining evidence from reliable and credible sources. However, to use the databases effectively, you need to be familiar with the various research features, vocabulary, and techniques for researching and acquiring information. We offer the following suggestions to help you use databases effectively.

Tips for Using Databases

First, identify the key terms and/or vocabulary of the argument in order to have the proper language to use to research the topic. Sometimes basic research (from a tertiary source) is needed to discover the terms or vocabulary that is used in discussing the topic. Another way to identify the key terms is to make an initial search using a database and determine what topics are categorized in the results. For example, a student attempted to find research on the topic of animal abuse. When she did an initial search using the term "animal abuse," she discovered that the topic used terms such as "animal welfare" and "animal rights." In addition, the student discovered that there was a journal entitled, *Society & Animals* that focused specifically on animal issues such as animal abuse. By using the terms "animal welfare" and "animal rights," she discovered she was able to find the necessary sources and evidence for her presentation. In each case, the key to finding information on the topic was to identify the terms that are used to categorize the topic.

Second, become familiar with research databases and the types of information they provide. Each database has strengths and weaknesses depending on the type of information needed. For example, *CQ Researcher* is a valuable database that provides articles and commentary on contemporary issues and is a great source for identifying the major arguments for and against an issue. *LexisNexis* is a vital database that covers legal and business topics and is a good source for finding legal (court cases) and economic evidence related to a topic. Regardless of the type of database you use, it is important to understand the variations in how it is used to find research, including the use of search terms and the narrowing and expansion of a search.

Third, review information. A common mistake made is not carefully reviewing the information once it is acquired. Reviewing information lets you discover the following: 1) the type of evidence you acquired; 2) how the information supports your arguments; 3) whether the information relates to the topic; 4) whether the information relates to the audience; and 5) the reliability of the information. These are all important questions that you need to determine before deciding if you are finished researching a topic. Too often, individuals wait until the last moment to obtain information, which leaves little or no time to scrutinize and evaluate the adequacy of the evidence. All research should be done early enough to ascertain the necessity of additional research.

Up to this point, we have discussed the different types of evidence, some guidelines for their use along with categorizing evidence to determine its strength. We also briefly discussed how to conduct and acquire research. Next, we will discuss how to test evidence to ensure that you receive the most reliable and verifiable information to back up your claims.

EVALUATING EVIDENCE

The evidence speakers find is only as good as the sources in which it is obtained. If the evidence a speaker acquires cannot be verified, it can undermine a speaker's credibility and argument. When evidence is retrieved, it must be tested and evaluated before it is used as support for an argument. We discuss some of the most important tests of evidence that speakers need to address in order to recognize and identify sound evidence, which includes the following: credibility, bias, currency, consistency, completeness, and corroboration.

Tests of Evidence

Credibility. When speakers acquire information, they will need to determine the credibility of the source. Does the source have the background, knowledge, expertise, and integrity (ethics) to produce the information that was obtained? One way to check the credibility of the source is to research the author's background, education, accomplishments, and awards. In addition, speakers should check the primary and secondary sources the author uses along with determining the purpose and goal of the information. If the source's or author's credibility can be verified, then the evidence obtained will be much more reliable and trustworthy.

Sometimes, credibility is determined by time. For example, information from established news sources tends to be more credible because they have a track record for providing reliable information. However, information should not be taken blindly because there can be inaccuracies even in established sources, which is why speakers always need to verify and corroborate evidence with other sources.

Bias. In the media age, it is becoming increasingly more difficult to identify source bias due to the subtlety in which bias is presented in a source. For this reason, it is important to know the self-interests of the source, which could result in biased reporting. For example, a source opposing or advocating a position on a controversial topic like gun control, abortion, or Internet regulation might be receiving substantial political support from the respective interest groups promoting one side or the other.

Currency. Currency refers to the recency of information. There is a tendency to believe that the more up to date information is, the better it is. If a speaker were arguing against new standards for food in high schools but uses evidence from 10 years ago, the argument would be weak because the evidence is not recent. Recency, however, also refers to the speaker being aware of current issues, new procedures, and ongoing cases related to the argument. For example, if a speaker were arguing for the inclusion of special-needs children in regular classrooms but did not cite an ongoing local case involving a special-needs child, it would illustrate that the speaker was not current with the issue. In this case, the speaker missed an opportunity to demonstrate that she "did her homework" and was aware of various aspects of the issue. In sum, currency suggests that the speaker has retrieved the current (and accurate) information and is aware of current issues related to the argument.

Consistency. If the source does not contain any contradictions, the source has consistency. Consistency deals with the absence of contradictions in the same document (or within a campaign). This is different from using statements from a person at one time in life and then another, because it is common for people to change their minds over the years. In contrast, a contradiction in a single document weakens a speaker's argument. For example, if a speaker used a quotation from an official to support a claim, and the speaker's opponent used a quotation from the same official and from the same document to make an opposing argument, it would severely undermine the speaker's argument. The speaker should have reviewed the document carefully in an effort to determine if any contradiction was present. Often, the contradiction might not be apparent until the speaker reviews the primary source in which the evidence was gathered (which is another reason primary sources are important to acquire).

Completeness. Another test of evidence involves completeness. This refers to whether the source of the evidence (or the evidence provided in the argument) provides enough information for a reasonable person to accept. For example, if the source supported inclusion by arguing that it is every student's right to be in a regular classroom, the argument as presented would not be complete enough. The source would need to include additional information like providing some support material (facts and statistics) to demonstrate that it is feasible and that the teachers have the training and assistance to handle special-needs children in a regular classroom. In this case, the source provided enough evidence that a reasonable person can at least understand how inclusion could work. Again, critical thinking skills are necessary to review information to decide if enough evidence is presented to support the claim.

Corroboration. Corroboration refers to whether other credible and reliable sources agree with the source's claims and the source's evidence. In other words, corroboration enables speakers to verify the accuracy of evidence. When speakers are able to demonstrate that other sources agree with their evidence, it bolsters the claims they are making.

All of these tests of evidence help speakers to determine the strength (or weakness) of their evidence. Passing these tests is important because even the failure of a single test of evidence might create enough doubt with the audience to undermine a speaker's position. Likewise, speakers need to be very careful when considering web pages as sources in a debate. Web pages should undergo the same tests of evidence that we have mentioned along with some additional tests that we discuss next.

Tests of Evidence for Web Pages

As we have mentioned earlier, web pages are often poor sources of evidence because they do not stand up to the tests of evidence presented above. When individuals are browsing web pages, it is not as systematic or as reliable as information gained from databases.

Regarding online research, evidence that is acquired from databases or from online newspapers is more credible than is evidence obtained from the web. Web pages require more scrutiny because, oftentimes, the information cannot be verified to be true, is often inaccurate, biased, or not up to date. Be cautioned that even online newspapers and official web sites are often wrong or inaccurate due to the emphasis placed on the speed with which the information is posted instead of its accuracy. All of the tests of evidence we have mentioned also apply to web pages and online sources. Briefly, we discuss how some of the tests of evidence can be used to evaluate web pages.

The credibility of the web page should be thoroughly evaluated. Who wrote the page? What is their authority? What are the source's credentials? How does the source or author indicate his/her experience? Does the web page refer to credible primary sources? Is the web connected to a credible source? These questions point to the difficulty in "nailing down" information on the credibility of the source. What does the URL (web address) say about the source of the web site and its purpose? For example, .gov (government) sources tend to be more credible than .net (Internet) or .com (commercial site) sources. However, even when the URL is known, the other tests of evidence for credibility are difficult to administer.

Oftentimes, when the credibility of the source can be determined, it reveals that the source is created for a particular purpose, which reveals the bias of the source. The danger is for the speaker to take the information as true when the information on the web site is slanted for a particular cause or purpose. Furthermore, primary sources or even secondary sources might be referred to, but commonly, the evidence is manipulated, omitted, or distorted in ways that support the cause or purpose but do not provide an accurate understanding of the topic or issue.

Speakers should be aware of the currency of the web page. What is the date of the web page? Has it been updated? How old is the information contained on the web page? If you cannot determine when the information was posted, then it can't be very useful in a debate. In addition, speakers should evaluate the consistency and completeness of the web page. Again, just because information is presented on a web page does not mean it is consistent or complete; speakers need to use their critical thinking skills to evaluate these tests of evidence. Finally, does the information on the web page corroborate other credible and reliable sources? If not, the information is not likely to be accurate.

Tests of Evidence for Cultural Beliefs

Another test of evidence that is important to consider is whether cultural beliefs influence the acceptance of sources or evidence used in a debate. As we have discussed in Chapter 1, the cultural lens in which we perceive reality can shape our interpretation and attribution of meaning. The cultural lens can be defined by nationality, region, or ethnicity. For example, the news coverage of the war with Iraq is very different when comparing the American press to the Arab press. One of the main differences is that the Arab press tends to focus on the death of civilians at the hands of an "occupier," while the American press emphasizes American soldier deaths (without showing the graphic details).[8]

Within the United States, various cocultures can have different cultural perspectives. For example, African-American culture often views law enforcement differently from the dominant culture. In the dominant culture, the emphasis is often placed on the action and the type of punishment the individual should receive. In contrast, the focus in African-American culture tends to be on the treatment of the person who was arrested. These perceptions are directly opposite one another due, in large part, to the experience each culture has had with law enforcement. The result of these contrasting cultural perspectives is the dominant culture tends to trust law enforcement whereas African-American culture does not.[9]

When acquiring evidence and contemplating sources, the speaker needs to be conscious of how the audience perceives sources and evidence. If a speaker uses a quotation from an officer to support a claim when addressing a predominantly African-American audience, the quotation will probably receive more scrutiny than if the audience were mostly white. Likewise, a conservative, rural audience would perceive the National Rifle Association (NRA) as a credible source on the issue of gun control while a more liberal, metropolitan audience would probably perceive the NRA in a different light. These examples underlie the principle that the credibility of a source varies from audience to audience based upon the audience members' cultural beliefs and values.

SUMMARY

We began this chapter by referring to the importance of using and testing evidence in order to support claims within a speech. Thus, speakers need to be able to use research databases to obtain reliable evidence from primary and secondary sources. Furthermore, to ensure that evidence is reliable, speakers must test and evaluate it before it can be used as support for an argument. Finally, speakers should cite the source from which the evidence was retrieved.

NOTES

1 Toulmin, S. (1976). *Knowing and acting* (p. 138). New York, NY: Macmillan.
2 Priest, D., & Pincus, W. (2004, October 7). U.S. "almost all wrong" on weapons; report on Iraq contradicts Bush administration claims. *The Washington Post*, p. AO1.
3 See Inch, E., & Warnick, B. (1989). *Critical thinking and communication: The use of reason in argument* (3rd ed.). Boston, MA: Allyn & Bacon.

4 See Fisher, W. (1987). *Human communication as narration: Toward a philosophy of reason, value, and action*. Columbia: South Carolina Press.

5 Larson, C. (2001). *Persuasion: Reception and responsibility* (9th ed.). Belmont, CA: Wadsworth.

6 See Rohler, L., & Cook, R. (1998). *Great speeches for criticism & speeches* (3rd ed.). Greenwood, IN: Alistair Press.

7 Ibid.

8 Gilgoff, D. (2003, April 7). Everybody's watching, but on different channels. *U.S. News & World Report*, p. 50.

9 See Hurwitz, J., & Peffley, M. (2005). Explaining the great racial divide: Perceptions of fairness in the U.S. criminal justice system. *Journal of Politics, 67*(3), 762–783.

Chapter 5

Analyzing Propositions

CHAPTER OUTLINE

KEY TERMS

Burden of Proof
Burden of Rejoinder
Conceptual Definition
Criteria
Cost
Inherency
Issues
Operational Definition
Plan
Presumption

Prima Facie Case
Proposition
Proposition of Fact
Proposition of Value
Proposition of Policy
Significance
Status Quo
Stock Issues
Topicality
Workability

The first formal presidential debates in America took place in 1858 between an ex-congressman and a senator, both from Illinois. In these extraordinary Lincoln–Douglas debates, the first candidate spoke for 60 minutes, the second candidate spoke for 90 minutes, and the first candidate closed the debate with a 30-minute rebuttal. Much has changed in the modern age of television. Opening speeches in the first televised presidential debates between Kennedy and Nixon were 8 minutes. But even that might seem long-winded compared to the 3 minutes allowed in the Ford–Carter debates, and the mere 2 minutes allowed in presidential debates since 1976.[1]

In this chapter, we begin discussing the practice of debate, the primary public speaking context in which argumentation occurs. In Chapter 1, we identified two essential features of a formal debate: following established rules, and arguing for and against a **proposition**, which is a statement of belief put to debate. Interestingly, while all presidential debates follow set rules, agreed to by the parties involved, none requires the participants to speak for or against a particular proposition. Thus, strictly speaking, presidential "debates" are not debates at all, according to most definitions of that term.[2]

The practice of debate begins by declaring a proposition, letting the participants know what they will be arguing for or against. At that point, the participants can take the first step, analyzing the proposition. Just as we analyze an argument by taking it apart and studying the parts (e.g., claim, grounds, reasoning), we analyze a proposition by taking it apart and studying its parts. But what are the "parts" of a proposition? As you will see in this chapter, the parts of a proposition are known as **issues**—important questions that frame key points of disagreement. But before we discuss the analysis of a proposition, we need to consider the task of selecting a proposition for debate

THE NATURE OF DEBATE PROPOSITIONS

As noted above, a proposition is a statement of belief chosen as a topic for debate. This definition distinguishes a proposition from a simple claim. While a claim is also a statement of belief, it serves only as part of an argument (see Chapter 2). But when a claim becomes the topic of a debate, we refer to the claim, more formally, as a proposition. For example, in the argument that cigarette smoking is harmful to your health because it causes lung cancer, the claim is that *cigarette smoking is harmful to your health*. The grounds (premise) in the argument are that *cigarette smoking causes lung cancer*. If we select this claim as the topic for a debate where one or more speakers will try to prove that the claim is true, and one or more speakers will try to prove that the claim is false, then the claim becomes a proposition.

But all claims are not worthy of debate and do not make good propositions. What are the requirements for a good proposition? First, a proposition needs to be controversial; reasonable people should be able to make strong arguments both for and against the proposition. There is little need to debate a one-sided proposition, since the preponderance of evidence already favors one side and the "truth" of the proposition may be readily apparent. Additionally, a "lopsided" debate is not likely to generate much interest; nor is it likely to hold the attention of an audience. Finally, if a proposition is not two-sided, it puts one side at a serious disadvantage, making it more difficult for speakers representing that side to put together a convincing case. Based on this guideline, would the claim that *cigarette smoking is harmful to your health* make a suitable topic for debate? We think not.

The second requirement is that a proposition should contain a single belief. A proposition containing two beliefs is, by definition, two propositions incorrectly stated as one. Ultimately, we debate a proposition as a way of determining whether it is true or not. If a proposition contains two different beliefs, we may find that one of those beliefs is true while the other belief is not. For instance, consider the proposition that *the amount of sex and violence on television is increasing*. Although the proposition may be controversial, it contains more than a single belief. Perhaps, after weighing all the evidence, we find that violence on television is increasing but the amount of sex on television is not. This is why in science a researcher tests one hypothesis at a time, in the courtroom a judge rules on one charge at a time, and in the legislature, members of congress debate one proposal at a time.

The third requirement is that a proposition should advocate a change in belief. In fact, the desire for change is the impetus for debate, the driving force behind the need to "test" new ideas and policies. A contemporary example is the debate on whether the federal government should fund embryonic stem cell research. Would there be any debate if no one put forth a proposition advocating change, suggesting that stem cell research has the potential to cure a host of diseases? Requiring a proposition to advocate a change in belief is a way of getting an audience to question and perhaps consider changing existing beliefs, values, and policies, a prerequisite for progress. Thus, debate becomes a way of checking the viability of the **status quo**, holding it accountable: should we continue on our present course or is it time to chart a new course? And the goal of the advocate is not merely to affirm the status quo but to challenge it. From an educational standpoint, debate develops skills in advocacy, and advocating a change in belief is much more demanding than is advocating a prevailing belief, controversial though it may be.

The fourth requirement is that a proposition should not express a bias toward one side or the other. It should not contain any implicit and unfair assumptions. For example, do you detect any bias in the following propositions?

1. *The federal government should eliminate unnecessary social programs*
2. *The liberal media promotes political correctness in its coverage of the news*
3. *The pseudoscience of Intelligent Design should be taught in our schools*

Proposition number 1 advocates eliminating *unnecessary* social programs, which biases the proposition in favor of the advocate. After all, if a program is unnecessary, it should be eliminated. But a fair debate would include arguments about whether certain social programs are in fact unnecessary. Similarly, proposition number 2 claims that the *liberal* media promotes political correctness. Since we associate political correctness with liberals rather than with conservatives, the assumption of a "liberal" media biases the proposition in favor of the advocate, rendering the proposition unfit for debate. On the other hand, we could debate whether or not the media is liberal, and we could debate whether or not the media promotes political correctness in its news coverage, but these are two different propositions. Finally, by calling intelligent design a *pseudoscience*, proposition number 3 clearly favors the side against teaching intelligent design over the side in favor of teaching it.

TYPES OF DEBATE PROPOSITIONS

By meeting the four requirements noted above, we could put forth a proposition suitable for debate. But analyzing the proposition, focusing on the *issues,* depends on the type of proposition we choose. In this section, we discuss three distinct types: propositions of fact, propositions of value, and propositions of policy.

Propositions of Fact

A **proposition of fact** asserts the existence of something in the past, present, or future. A distinguishing feature is that these propositions are verifiable. That is, through direct observation we can determine, within reason, whether the proposition probably is true or false. Of course, if a proposition is easy to verify, it won't be controversial enough to debate. We might argue, for a short time, over whether the unemployment rate increased last month, or whether this summer's box office gross exceeds last summer's, but a simple matter of checking the facts will put an end to the dispute.

In contrast, a good proposition of fact will provoke and sustain debate over time. For instance, the proposition that *global warming will increase the risk of wildfires* is a specific claim about the effects of global warming on the environment that researchers can verify, even though they may disagree about what they discover after using well-known and accepted methods of inquiry. Not surprisingly, debates on propositions of fact ultimately boil down to disputes over which side is presenting the best available research.

Propositions of Value

A **proposition of value**, simply stated, asserts the relative worth (value) of something, rather than the mere existence of something. These propositions claim that something is good or bad, right or wrong, better or worse, and so forth. Unlike propositions of fact, value propositions are not amenable to the methods of empirical research—we cannot verify the truth of the proposition through direct observation. Instead, we rely on factual claims supported by direct observation to build our case for or against propositions of value. Continuing with the topic of global warming, a value proposition is that *global warming is the most urgent problem facing the world today*. Every proposition of value contains a ***value object***, which is the thing being evaluated, and a ***value term***, the positive or negative value attributed to the value object.[3] In our example, "global warming" is the value object and "most urgent problem" is the value term. Because values are not directly verifiable, propositions of value generally make better debate topics than do propositions of fact.

Propositions of Policy

A **proposition of policy** asserts that something should be done; it recommends a course of action (policy). An example of a policy proposition on the topic of global warming is that *the federal government should enact new measures to significantly reduce greenhouse emissions*. There are two important features of policy propositions that facilitate the task of analysis. The first is that they indicate a reasonably clear change in policy. In our example, the advocate is calling for new measures to significantly reduce greenhouse emissions, which could include various plans to conserve energy and develop safer energy sources. The second feature is that they designate a ***change agent***, the entity responsible for initiating the proposed change in policy. In our example, the change agent is the federal government.

The type of proposition chosen for a debate will shape the kind of analysis that must be done. But the task of analyzing a proposition must await the assignment of sides: an advocate who speaks in favor of the proposition, and an opponent who speaks against it. In the next section, we briefly consider how the two sides approach the task of analysis.

ADVOCACY AND DEBATE PROPOSITIONS

In a debate, taking sides carries certain obligations. Most fundamentally, the side advocating the proposition—called the "affirmative" side in academic debates—has the **burden of proof**, the obligation to initiate debate by offering convincing arguments in favor of the proposition. Failure to meet this burden of proof means that the advocate failed to present a **prima facie case**, which is a set of arguments sufficient "on its first appearance" to convince a reasonable person that the proposition is probably true.

At this point you may be wondering why the side advocating a proposition has the burden of proof. The reason is that debate propositions call for a change in beliefs, values, or policies and, for the most part, people do not willfully change what they think or do without sufficient cause. This bias in favor of the status quo affords the opponent an edge in the debate known as

presumption. The advocate's challenge is to overcome this bias (presumption) with strong and compelling arguments. Thus, from an educational standpoint, we regard academic debate primarily as training in advocacy, which is why your participation in debate will require you to switch sides so that every participant has an opportunity to construct and present a prima facie case.

If the advocate in a debate has the burden of proof, what then is the primary obligation of the opponent (the "negative" side in an academic debate)? At the start of the debate, we give the opponent the benefit of presumption; we accept the status quo until convinced otherwise. This practice relies on the same cautious decision-making used in other fields, where rigorous argumentation is the accepted way of seeking the truth, such as in science where researchers do not hastily endorse new theories, and in law where juries do not hastily convict defendants: the "status quo" is presumed "innocent" until proven otherwise based on some accepted standard of proof.

But after the advocate offers a prima facie case, the opponent has the equally important **burden of rejoinder**, requiring the opponent to challenge the advocate's arguments and to prove that the advocate's case does not constitute sufficient grounds for the proposition.

In academic debate, the advocate of change usually has the burden of proof, and the opponent usually has the benefit of presumption. But determining which side in a dispute has the burden of proof and which side has presumption is less settled, though no less important, in some debating contexts than in others (see Chapter 9). For instance, in the "court of public opinion," we often give the benefit of presumption to the side expressing beliefs, values, and policies most closely aligned with those of the greatest number of people.

Even in the courtroom, questions can arise over which side in a dispute has the burden of proof. One recent court case on this issue did not get settled until reaching the U.S. Supreme Court. The case focused on who had the burden of proof in school disputes concerning the Individuals with Disabilities Education Act. Arguing against a lower court ruling, the National Education Association (NEA) claimed that educators should not have the burden of proving that a particular Individualized Educational Program (IEP) is appropriate for a child with a disability, but rather that parents who reject the IEP must prove that it is not appropriate for their child.

Ultimately, the Supreme Court endorsed the NEA position and ruled that parents, not school officials, have the burden of proving a parent's claim that an IEP for a child with a disability does not satisfy the child's needs.

Justice Sandra Day O'Connor wrote for the majority: "The burden of persuasion in an administrative hearing challenging an IEP is properly placed on the party seeking relief, whether that is the disabled child or the school district."

The Court maintained that the "complaining" or "challenging" party (opposing the status quo) owns the burden of proof. If parents claim that an IEP is not appropriate, then they have the burden to prove it is not appropriate. If the school district claims that a child's education is not appropriate, then the district has the burden of proof.[4]

A clear understanding of who has the burden of proof in a debate is an essential starting point. The next task is to begin analyzing the issues contained in the proposition.

GENERAL ANALYSIS OF DEBATE PROPOSITIONS

The key issues contained in a given proposition are called **stock issues**, which are a set of questions that must be answered as the advocate builds a prima facie case. Stock issues provide clear guidelines for determining whether or not an advocate has met the burden of proof in a dispute.

Although stock issues vary with different types of propositions, there are three "generic" issues central to all propositions in any context:

1. What are we trying to prove (defining terms)?
2. How do we know if it's true (identifying the criteria)?
3. Is it true (applying the criteria)?

These issues represent fundamental questions pertinent to any kind of dispute, and the more formal the dispute is the more important these questions become for those charged with the responsibility of rendering an objective decision. To illustrate, the judge in a criminal trial will urge a jury to fully comprehend the charge against a defendant (defining terms), the standard of proof needed for conviction (identifying a criteria), and the evidence offered by the attorneys (applying the criteria).

Defining Terms

The advocate has the responsibility of clarifying the proposition, thereby "setting the stage" for debate on all other issues. In a criminal case, the "charge" brought against a defendant represents a factual proposition—the topic of debate for opposing attorneys. Critical to the outcome of the trial is a clear understanding of the charge. For example, in a murder trial, what does it mean to be charged with "first-degree murder"? Although the legal definition varies slightly from state to state, first-degree murder is the deliberate, premeditated, and unlawful taking of another life.[5] This definition informs everyone involved of what the prosecutor (advocate) will try to prove.

Likewise, in the context of academic debate, the advocate of a proposition must define key terms so that everyone knows what the advocate will actually try to prove. A key term is one that is central to our understanding of the proposition. Of course, some key terms require definitions more than others do. In their book, *Advocacy and Opposition*, Karyn and Donald Rybacki suggest defining the following terms:

- *Equivocal terms* have two or more equally correct meanings
- *Vague terms* have shades of meaning; they lack clear-cut definitions
- *Technical terms* are jargon or specialized words belonging to a particular field or profession
- *New terms* are recent additions to the language, words or phrases that do not exist in the common vocabulary
- *Coined terms* are those invented when a convenient term does not already exist.[6]

The meaning of a key term in some propositions can itself become the primary issue in a debate, fueling more controversy than we might have expected. For example, ongoing debate on the policy of using torture as an interrogation tactic in the war on terror has spawned considerable disagreement over what "torture" means under such circumstances, and whether the United States endorses torture or not.

The United Nations defines torture as "any act by which severe pain or suffering, whether physical or mental, is intentionally inflicted on a person for such purposes as obtaining from him or a third

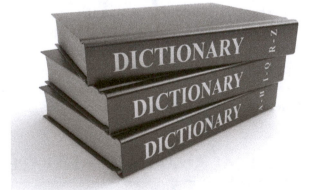

One of the key responsibilities of an advocate in any debate is to define the terms contained in the debate proposition.

person information or a confession, punishing him for an act he or a third person has committed or is suspected of having committed, or intimidating or coercing him or a third person, or for any reason based on discrimination of any kind, when such pain or suffering is inflicted by or at the instigation of or with the consent or acquiescence of a public official or other person acting in an official capacity."[7]

Under the Bush administration, the controversy centered on how far it could go legally in "aggressively interrogating" individuals suspected of terrorist activity or of having information that could thwart future terrorist attacks. In other words, when does aggressive interrogation end and torture begin?

The Bush Administration argued that moderate or fleeting pain is not necessarily torture. Instead, torture "must be equivalent in intensity to the pain accompanying serious physical injury, such as organ failure, impairment of bodily function, or even death."

In contrast, the Army's definition of torture includes "pain induced by chemicals or bondage; forcing an individual to stand, sit or kneel in abnormal positions for prolonged periods of time; and food deprivation. Under the category of mental torture, the Army prohibits "mock executions, sleep deprivation, and chemically induced psychosis."

But the Justice Department counters, "It is difficult to take a specific act out of context and conclude that the act in isolation would constitute torture." It lists seven techniques that courts have considered torture, including severe beatings with truncheons and clubs, threats of imminent death, burning with cigarettes, electric shocks to genitalia, rape or sexual assault, and forcing a prisoner to watch the torture of another person.[8]

Debate over the meaning of torture, which is not likely to end any time soon, shows how the use of vague and equivocal terms fosters disagreement, even among authoritative sources. In an academic debate, we refer to this particular issue as **topicality**, the question of whether the advocate's definitions offer a correct or reasonable interpretation of the proposition (topic) chosen for debate.

Identifying the Criteria

The next major issue raises the question: how do we know if the proposition is true? We call this the **criteria** issue because it requires the advocate to identify, and defend if necessary, some set of standards that will determine whether or not the advocate has met the burden of proof in any dispute. In other words, what is the *decision-making model* for determining the outcome of the dispute?

The courtroom again provides a good illustration. It isn't enough for a jury to understand what the charge of "first-degree murder" means. To reach a just verdict, the members must also understand, as precisely as possible, what the prosecutor must prove. In this case, what actions are sufficient to constitute the deliberate, premeditated, and unlawful killing of another person (i.e., the grounds), and how much evidence is needed for conviction (i.e., standard of proof)? Aside from demonstrating that the defendant intended to kill the

Applying some reasonable criteria, an advocate must satisfy the burden of proof. In a criminal trial, for example, the prosecutor must prove beyond a reasonable doubt that the defendant is guilty of the charge.

victim, the prosecutor must prove that enough time elapsed between the alleged murderer's intent to kill the victim and the actual killing, for some degree of planning to have occurred. However, most states also abide by a legal standard known as the "felony murder rule," under which a person can be charged with first-degree murder if a death occurs (even by accident) during the commission of a serious violent felony, such as armed robbery, arson, rape, or kidnapping.[9]

In a criminal case, the prosecutor must prove *beyond a reasonable doubt* that the defendant is guilty of the charge. Although it doesn't require absolute certainty, this is our legal system's highest standard of proof, requiring evidence of "such a convincing character that you would be willing to rely and act upon it without hesitation in the most important of your own affairs."[10] In most civil cases, a much lower standard of proof requires only that the plaintiff (advocate) support his or her position by the *preponderance of the evidence*, meaning that the proposition is more likely to be true than not true. An intermediate standard of proof, called *clear and convincing evidence*, requires the advocate to show that there is a high degree of probability that the proposition is true.

Applying the Criteria

After defining key terms and identifying appropriate criteria, the advocate begins the task of applying the criteria, which includes constructing a prima facie case and planning the presentation of that case to an audience. Continuing with our example of a murder trial, the prosecutor (advocate) must gather enough evidence (burden of proof) to convince a jury (audience), beyond a reasonable doubt (criteria/standard of proof), that the defendant is guilty of the charge of first-degree murder (proposition). In a criminal case, the prosecutor tries to construct a plausible narrative of what happened, offering evidence pertinent to the events leading up to and including the criminal act; and then plans how to present the evidence in the most persuasive way possible to the jury.

In an academic debate, the tasks of gathering evidence, constructing a convincing case, and then presenting that case to an audience depend on a variety of factors (see Chapters 4, 6 and 7). One of these factors, which we briefly address below, is the type of proposition—fact, value, or policy—chosen for debate.

SPECIFIC ANALYSIS OF DEBATE PROPOSITIONS

Regardless of which type of proposition we debate, a prima facie case requires an advocate to define key terms contained in the proposition, identify the criteria for determining the truth of the proposition, and then apply the criteria to the construction and presentation of arguments before audience members who decide the outcome of the debate. But how does our analysis of these issues differ for each type of proposition? Using the "global warming" topic we discussed earlier, let's consider what you would do as the advocate for each type of proposition

Stock Issues for Propositions of Fact

As we noted earlier, a proposition of fact is a verifiable claim asserting the existence of something in the past, present, or future. Our example was the proposition that *global warming will increase the risk of wildfires.*

■ What Does the Proposition Mean?

The first step in your analysis is to define key terms in the proposition. What does "global warming" mean? *The American Heritage Dictionary* defines it as "a gradual increase in the average temperature of the Earth's atmosphere, especially a sustained increase sufficient to cause climate change."[11] In addition, it defines the term "wildfire" as a raging, rapidly spreading fire.

■ What Criteria Determine the Truth of the Proposition?

The second step in your analysis is to determine the essential elements of a prima facie case. In other words, as the advocate, what is your burden of proof? Our factual proposition asserts a cause–effect relationship between global warming and an increased risk of wildfires. It also predicts that this will happen sometime in the future, implying that there are "signs" it will happen. The criteria for establishing a cause–effect relationship between two events include being able to prove that (1) there is a correlation between the two events (i.e., the occurrence of one event predicts the occurrence of the other event), (2) the alleged cause precedes the alleged effect, and (3) a third event is not responsible for the correlation between the two events.

■ Is the Proposition True?

Applied to our proposition, the criteria noted above means that in order to have a prima facie case you would need convincing evidence that (1) gradual increases in the temperature of the Earth's atmosphere have been associated with increased wildfires, (2) these temperature increases are a cause and not a consequence of more wildfires, and (3) the gradual increase in the temperature of the Earth's atmosphere and the increased occurrence of wildfires are not both being affected in a similar way by some other factor (e.g., increased lightning strikes, volcanic activity, etc.). In addition, you would need to prove that observable and reliable signs indicate that global warming is occurring or will occur in the future.

Stock Issues for Propositions of Value

A proposition of value is a claim asserting the relative worth of something. Unlike propositions of fact, value propositions are subjective and not verifiable through direct observation. The example we introduced earlier was the proposition that *global warming is the most urgent problem facing the world today.*

■ What Does the Proposition Mean?

You begin your analysis by identifying and defining the value object and the value term. In this proposition, the **value object** is "global warming," which we defined above. The **value term** is the judgment expressed in the proposition about the value object: global warming is "the most urgent problem" facing the world today. What is a reasonable interpretation of this value term? First, you can define a "problem" as "an obstacle which makes it difficult to achieve a desired goal, objective, or purpose. It refers to a situation, condition, or issue that is yet unresolved."[12] Second, the term "urgent" refers to something requiring immediate attention. Finally, the term "most" means that no other problem facing the world today requires more immediate attention than does global warming.

■ What Criteria Determine the Truth of the Proposition?

Based on the definitions above, how will you prove that global warming is the most urgent problem facing the world today? The proposition requires some basis for making comparisons among various problems facing the world today, some set of standards for "ranking" global warming as the most urgent of all problems. You could claim, for instance, that a reasonable criterion for making such a determination is that the most urgent problem should be the most imminent threat to the survival of our species.

■ Is the Proposition True?

Having offered a standard for making comparisons among problems facing the world today, the next step is to develop a prima facie case for the proposition. Thus, you would need to gather evidence clearly showing that no other problem facing the world today poses a more imminent threat to the survival of our species. This criterion requires evidence that the consequences of global warming are not only capable of destroying all human life but also that they are more immediate than those of other similarly devastating problems. Consequences of such magnitude sometimes attributed to global warming include drought, spread of disease, famine, and flooding.[13]

Stock Issues for Propositions of Policy

As we noted earlier, a proposition of policy asserts that something should be done; it advocates a course of action. Our example was the proposition that *the federal government should enact new measures to significantly reduce greenhouse emissions.*

■ What Does the Proposition Mean?

In this proposition, the term "greenhouse emissions" clearly stands out as a technical term you need to define. The term refers to atmospheric gases that absorb solar infrared radiation, contributing to the "greenhouse effect" that traps heat and raises the Earth's temperature. Greenhouse emissions that increase levels of carbon dioxide in the atmosphere are most significant and include those released from fossil fuel production, automobiles, and various other sources.[14]

When we use a dictionary or some other source to clarify the meaning of a term, as we have been doing so far, we get a **conceptual definition** of the term (i.e., words, phrases, and statements that define the term). But conceptual definitions lack the specificity we need when clarifying policy propositions because they do not tell us what the advocate is proposing to do, which lies at the heart of all policy propositions. In other words, what is the advocate's **plan**? The advocate offers an **operational definition** of the proposition in the form of a plan that spells out, in some reasonable detail, what the advocate thinks should be done by the change agent specified in the proposition. In our example, what kinds of new measures should the federal government enact to significantly reduce greenhouse emissions? So your plan might include increased investments in alternative energy sources (solar, wind, geothermal, biomass, etc.), energy conservation, public transportation, and the like.

■ What Criteria Determine the Truth of the Proposition?

The most useful standard for determining the truth of a policy proposition, which always advocates a new course of action, is some type of cost-benefit analysis: Do the benefits of the plan outweigh the costs of the plan? In order to have a prima facie case, you must prove that benefits of your plan are more significant than the costs. This cost-benefit standard of proof produces what we call the "four stock issues criteria" of policy debate: significance, inherency, workability, and cost.

1. *Significance*—this issue requires the advocate to prove there is a "significant need" to change, such as solving a problem that is hurting many people, and/or draining highly valued resources.
2. *Inherency*—this issue requires the advocate to prove that the status quo (i.e., present policies) is not capable of meeting the need.

3. ***Workability***—this issue (sometimes called ***solvency***) requires the advocate to prove that the plan being proposed can do a better job of meeting the need than the status quo can.

4. ***Cost***—this issue (also called ***disadvantages***) requires the advocate to prove that any costs (or disadvantages) of the plan are outweighed by its benefits (i.e., removing or lessening a significant problem.

■ Is the Proposition True?

Let's suppose your operational definition of the proposition is a plan requiring automakers to manufacture more energy-efficient cars. How do you meet your burden of proof? Working with the four stock issues noted above, you would construct a case for the proposition (i.e., your plan) consisting of four main arguments: (1) Greenhouse emissions are creating significant problems today (e.g., flooding, drought, wildfires, etc.); (2) Current policies do not require automobile manufacturers to reduce their greenhouse emissions; (3) Requiring automobile manufacturers to produce more energy-efficient cars will greatly reduce greenhouse emissions; and (4) The disadvantages of requiring automakers to manufacture more energy-efficient cars are not as significant as are the benefits of requiring them to do so.

SUMMARY

In a debate, speakers argue for or against a proposition, a statement of belief chosen for debate. Good debate propositions should be controversial, contain a single belief, advocate a change in belief, and not express any bias toward one side or the other. We discussed three different types of propositions suitable for debate: a proposition of fact asserts the existence of something in the past, present, or future; propositions of value assert the relative worth of something (i.e., a value judgment); and propositions of policy offer a new course of action.

The advocate (affirmative side) of a proposition has the burden of proof and therefore must present a prima facie case for the proposition. The opponent (negative side) of the proposition has the benefit of presumption, which favors the side defending the status quo. But once the advocate presents a prima facie case, the opponent has the burden of rejoinder, and needs to show that the advocate's case does not constitute sufficient grounds for the proposition. Analyzing a proposition means understanding the issues or main points of disagreement that can arise from debating the proposition. This includes the stock issues of defining key terms, identifying a criteria for determining the truth of the proposition, and the applying the criteria to the construction and presentation of a prima facie case. This analysis depends on whether a proposition is one of fact, value, or policy.

NOTES

1 Commission on Presidential Debates.
2 See for example Corcoran, J. M., Nelson, M., & Perella, J. (2006). *Critical thinking through debate*. Dubuque, IA: Kendall Hunt.
3 Rybacki, K. C., & Rybacki, D. J. (2004). *Advocacy and opposition*. Boston, MA: Allyn & Bacon.
4 See Wrightslaw.com for information on this case.
5 See lectlaw.com for this and other legal definitions.

6   Rybacki, & Rybacki. (2004).

7   See definitions of torture cited by Wikipedia.com.

8   Priest, D., & Smith, R. J. (2004, June 8). Memo ordered justification for use of torture. *Washington Post*, p. A01.

9   See definitions of first-degree murder cited by Wikipedia.com.

10 Retrieved from www.lectlaw.com

11 Retrieved from thefreedictionary.com

12 This is a typical definition of the term. Retrieved from wikipedia.com

13 Retrieved from http://www.nrdc.org/globalWarming/fcons.asp

14 Retrieved from http://www.greenhouse.nsw.gov.au/climate_change_in_nsw/emissions_nsw

Chapter 6

Constructing a Convincing Case

CHAPTER OUTLINE

KEY TERMS

Affirmative Case

Brainstorming

Contention

Comparative Advantages Case

Core Value

Counter Plan

Criteria Case

Evidence Card

Goals Case

Minor Repair

Need-Plan Case

Negative Case

Topicality Arguments

Value Hierarchy

There is an old *Peanuts* cartoon in which Lucy is preparing for a class debate. She is busily working when her brother Linus comes up and asks what she is doing. With tremendous confidence, Lucy responds, "I am going to be in a debate. These are some notes I'm preparing so I'll be ready." Lucy eagerly proceeds to show Linus her note cards, which read: "So? Who cares? Why not? Forget it!!! Oh, Yeah? Drop Dead!" Linus then responds weakly, "I think you're ready."

Unlike Lucy's preparation in this humorous illustration, realistic preparation for a classroom debate doesn't involve coming up with quips and insults to hurl at your opponents (as much as we all might like to do that). The level of preparation you will need to engage in will be time intensive and involve much research. However, if you know how to prepare in a systematic, organized method, your experience will be much less time consuming and frustrating.

In this chapter, we explain how to construct a convincing case to support or oppose a proposition. The case constructed by an advocate supporting the proposition is known as an **affirmative case,** whereas a **negative case** is a set of arguments put together by an opponent of the proposition. First, we discuss how to get your evidence ready for case construction and then we demonstrate how to write a case for and against a proposition.

PREPARATION FOR CONSTRUCTING A CASE

As we discussed in Chapter 4, debating a proposition usually requires extensive library research utilizing reference works, research databases, and the Internet to locate a variety of articles, books, documents, and papers. Interviews are often conducted. The results of this research are recorded, copied, paraphrased, and filed for future use in an orderly, highly systematic manner. This preparation phase, which can be quite time consuming, is one of the most essential elements of debating. Although strong, effective oral presentation skills are important, if debaters don't have the proper information to refute or support key arguments, they will lose the debate no matter how effective their delivery.

After some preliminary analysis of a debate proposition, including some initial library research, the task of case construction begins. A written case for or against a proposition may seem to be a daunting, if not impossible, task. But establishing a step-by-step process for constructing a case on a debate proposition is beneficial, and once that process becomes familiar, it can be used to construct a case on any proposition. The first step in this process, as you learned in preparing a speech, is brainstorming.

Brainstorming

Brainstorming is the process whereby new, different, or original ideas are generated. When starting work on a debate proposition, generating ideas is essential. To brainstorm, let your mind wander to consider all possible interpretations, issues, principles, and arguments relevant to the topic. The first key to successful brainstorming is interaction with others. Discuss ideas with other students, your instructor, friends, or relatives. The creative energy caused by this interaction will generate more ideas. The second key to brainstorming is to avoid ruling out ideas automatically because at first they are perceived as silly, wrong, weak, or unrealistic. After a more thorough examination, many of these ideas may lead to more legitimate and truly important points that you want to include in your case. Allow one idea to lead to others and allow yourself to branch out from what has been said. The brainstorming process is not designed to be efficient, but thorough—the more ideas the better. When it appears that all ideas have been generated, decide which ideas have the most merit. Explore these ideas more thoroughly.[1] In order to do this, you need to move to step 2 in the process: Defining terms in the proposition.

Defining Terms

As you learned in Chapter 5, one of the most important, yet frequently omitted, steps of the debate preparation process is defining terms in the proposition. Defining terms is critical to the research process because some or all of the terms in a proposition may be open to a good deal of interpretation. As a result, the focus of the debate can go in several different directions. To be truly prepared to debate means to be ready to debate all of the different interpretations of a proposition. Strategies in debating different interpretations of the proposition (debate topic) are referred to as topicality arguments.

Recording and Organizing Evidence

In Chapter 4, we discussed the types of sources you need to research in order to support your arguments and how to evaluate the quality of those sources as you attempt to gather information in

One of the most important and time-consuming steps in constructing a convincing case is recording and organizing evidence.

support or against a debate proposition. However, knowing what to look for is as essential to the discovery of supporting evidence as where to look for information. In this section, we offer some practical guidelines to assist you in getting the information you need to construct a convincing case, how to record that information, and how to "cut" evidence from an article or report to use in a debate.

The process of gathering evidence is extremely time-consuming, tedious, and may be frustrating; however, it can also be exciting and fun. Treat this process like a treasure hunt you competed in as a child. Think about where you can find the information you need. Who would have such information and who would likely write about this topic? For example, what state or federal government agencies would be the ones that would publish reports about the environment, the judicial system, foreign trade, or the military? When you actually discover the information you need, you will see it can be very exhilarating—like finding the treasure you hunted for as a child. If that information becomes pivotal in a judge's decision to vote for you at the end of a debate, the time and effort spent will be well worth it. Karyn and Donald Rybacki in their textbook, *Advocacy and Opposition* suggest that debaters follow a multistep research process[2]:

1. *Have a clear idea of the evidence needed.* The results of your brainstorming analysis in conjunction with your definition of terms should provide you the necessary general focus to begin to research. Attempt to discover what information is available by skimming summaries, prefaces, and opening paragraphs of the courses you find.

    Read for ideas as much as for examples, statistics, and opinions. Once you have perused the available literature, begin to search for more specific information. This is where the stock issues become vital to your research. Since most of you will be debating policy propositions, remember the *four stock issues criteria* explained in Chapter 5: What are the problems/harms associated with your topic and are these problems significant? Is the status quo capable of solving these problems/harms? If not, is there a better plan for solving such problems? Does that plan have significant drawbacks? Keep in mind that you can only be efficient in looking for evidence if you have a clear idea of what arguments you are trying to prove. Reading for ideas gives you a sense of what can be proven with the resources available to you and keeps you from wasting time looking for evidence that may not exist.

2. *Keep an annotative bibliography as you gather your sources.* As you consider each printed source, record the title, author, publisher, date, and page numbers (where pertinent) on 4 × 6-inch index cards (one per source). If you have books or pamphlets that you are listing on the index cards, it is a good idea to include library call numbers so that you can locate them again quickly if necessary. For electronic sources, do the same, but substitute the Uniform Resource Locator (URL) or Web address instead of the call number. In a couple of sentences, write down the viewpoint of the author, a summary of what the source contains, and your personal evaluation of it. The purpose of this bibliography card is to give you a general idea of what a source contains. You will need to organize these cards either by author, chronologically by date, or by topic.

3. Create evidence cards. An evidence card contains support for the arguments in your case. To create these cards, you need to write down specific facts and opinions from the sources you have collected in an organized system, which will allow you to find what you need when you are ready to construct your case. Again, use one index card for each piece of evidence (e.g., expert opinion, fact, statistics, etc.) supporting a claim. Each card should contain:

   • A heading (the *claim* the evidence is supporting)
   • The citation (source): Author's name, title of article/magazine or book, place and date of publication, and page number(s).
   • For Internet sources, the URL address and the date you recorded the information
   • The author's qualifications or credentials
   • Accurate and verbatim evidence

On the proposition that *The United States should significantly increase its security assistance to Cambodia,* an advocate would need evidence of a problem that warrants such assistance to Cambodia. Here is an example of an evidence card supporting the claim that landmines in Cambodia pose a serious problem:

Claim: Landmines cause civilian deaths and injuries.

Source: R. Willmington, (Dir. of Govt. Studies and Chair of the Comm. On Military Security in S.E. Asia—Author's qualifications), *Nadis, 2013, p. 108 (publication, date, and page number).*

Evidence: "Landmines kill or maim 25,000 to 30,000 people a year, 80 per cent of them civilians."

It is also likely that you will discover a research source that has several pieces of evidence on a single page or couple of pages that you will want to use to support your arguments. It may be more efficient to photocopy the pages, mark the information that appears useful by placing brackets around each piece of potential evidence (i.e., sentences and/or paragraphs) and cut the "marked" evidence out of the photocopied pages and tape it on an index card. If you use this method, don't forget to record the citation (author, source, date) and heading (claim) on the index card.

4. ***Organize and classify your index cards by issue and claim.*** Once you have recorded information on a number of cards, you will have to arrange the cards in a fashion that will make it easy to find a piece of evidence quickly when you need to retrieve it during a debate. You could easily end up with as many as 50 index cards containing evidence and you do not want to waste precious time during a debate, shuffling through all your cards to find one piece of information, only to reshuffle through them moments later to find another piece of information. An organizational system will help you avoid this. This is why, the claim at the top of each index card is so essential. Although you can use any organizational format you wish, an effective method is to organize your evidence by the four stock issues initially (harm/ significance, inherency, solvency, disadvantages). Once your case is written, however, you will find it most efficient to organize the evidence by your major contentions and subpoints outlined in your case. This will be explained more fully later in the chapter.

5. ***Record evidence that is on the opposite side of the proposition in a different color or different size index card.*** Many debate instructors require students to both advocate and oppose the same proposition; you may end up with evidence on both sides of a proposition. It is easy to end up with evidence that opposes the proposition mixed up with your information that supports it. To avoid this, try to use two different colors of index cards. If that is not possible, then use two different sizes of index cards. Finally, you may wish to highlight the topic headings of your evidence in different colors (yellow/blue) to keep the information accurately organized.

Although these guidelines for collecting evidence may seem like a great deal of extra work, we do not recommend taking shortcuts, particularly when your assignment requires in-depth research on a single proposition. Evidence is absolutely essential to effectively support your arguments. Having a workable system that enables you to quickly retrieve information when you need it is vital to your success in a debate.

GUIDELINES FOR CONSTRUCTING A CASE

After you have the evidence you need, the next step is to begin constructing a *case*—the written composition or speech containing the arguments for or against the proposition. Like any speech, you will need to have an introduction, a body, and a conclusion. First we will discuss guidelines for creating the introduction and conclusion. Second, we will offer guidelines for composing the body of the speech, which consists of contentions and supporting evidence.

Creating Introductions and Conclusions

Regardless of which side you are on, your speech should not jump immediately to the arguments in support of the proposition. Debate should always be a public speaking event and, like a public speech, the presentation of the opening of the case determines the audience's first impression of you. As you know from previous public speaking courses, any effective speech should begin with an introduction.

Your introduction should attempt to gain the audience's attention and establish interest before moving to a more formal position in the debate. For example, you may want to begin with a quote, a story, an example, or a startling statistic that supports one of your main arguments. The introduction concludes with a transition to a formal statement of the proposition. An example would be the following:

> "In 2250 B.C., the code of Hammurabi made selling something to a child without power of attorney a crime punishable by death. American society has always attempted to protect children from mistreatment. But there is one area in which America has failed to protect its young—television advertising. Because of the government's lack of concern in this area, I support the proposition: *The federal government should significantly strengthen the regulation of mass media communication.*"

Always state the specific debate proposition in your introduction. The proposition, exactly as worded, is the focus of debate for both sides. Do not paraphrase or reword the proposition. If you're the advocate say you support the proposition; if you're the opponent say you oppose it.

The next step is defining key terms in the proposition. You should define each term essential to understanding your interpretation of the proposition. Remember from Chapter 5 that there are several different ways to do this. The most common are defining each important term with a definition from the dictionary or defining each term *operationally* through the provisions of your proposed plan (on policy propositions). Defining terms operationally is very efficient and saves time to develop other arguments. After stating the proposition, you would simply state "all terms are defined operationally through our plan."

The final part of the introduction involves a preview of the primary arguments in your case, called **contentions.** Simply list the contentions you will develop in your case. This helps the audience and judges follow the logic of your position in the debate. To illustrate, here is what a speaker might say in a preview:

> "In order to show you that the proposition is true I will argue that children are seriously harmed by television advertising; that no local, state, or federal laws are in place to prohibit this practice; and finally, a proposal that bans television advertising directed at children will minimize young children's exposure to harmful messages broadcasted by the media."

In addition to a strong introduction, which gets everyone's attention and lays out your position on the proposition, you need an equally strong conclusion to reinforce your position and leave a lasting impression. At a minimum, this includes a summary of your contentions as well as an attention-getting close (e.g., story, startling fact, personal experience, rhetorical question, thought-provoking quotation, etc.).

Try to refer to the introduction of your case. Tie the position of your case to the point made by the analogy or story that started your side in the debate. For example:

> "In the affirmative case that I presented this afternoon, I have proven that television advertising is inherently deceptive for young children. It is pervasive in our children's lives. As a result, they learn poor eating habits and are unknowingly encouraged to spend money on items they don't really want. Furthermore, the Federal Trade Commission (FTC) is unable to regulate the advertising industry and unfortunately, advertising companies will not voluntarily regulate themselves. The only reasonable course of action is the affirmative plan, which bans this type of advertising to children. We no longer live in 2250 B.C. and have the Code of Hammurabi to protect our children. Therefore, we must act now and provide a new code of protection through the affirmative policy. It is only by voting affirmative at the end of today's debate that we can truly save America's youth from the travesty of television advertisements."

Developing Contentions

The body of the speech consists of contentions with supporting evidence. This part of your case should meet the requirements listed below:

- **All contentions should be numbered in the body of your speech** (Contention I., Contention II, etc.). This is important in helping the audience, the judges, and the other side follow the organizational structure of your case and quickly identify the arguments you are presenting.
- **Keep the contentions short, clear, and as simple as possible.** The other side and the judges will need to write down your contentions as you state them; therefore, keeping the contention clear and concise will assist them in this endeavor. For example, "The status quo cannot solve this problem because of a shortage of funding," is much easier to understand and write down than, "The status quo has many problems which preclude solvency of this situation including a lack of strong financial incentives and means." Remember, it is easier to have a good debate if both sides are organized and clear so that both sides are able to dispute each other's arguments.
- **Use subpoints when two or more claims provide support for a contention.** Because it is impossible to divide something into fewer than two parts, always remember that if you are dividing a contention, you will need at least two subpoints to support the contention. The rule to follow is: never "I" without "II," never "A" without "B," and so on.
- **Use parallel wording for the contentions and subpoints whenever possible.** Again, it makes the case easier to understand and follow. Parallel wording means that your contentions should

be worded in a similar or "parallel" manner. For example, if you were arguing a policy proposition calling for the elimination of capital punishment, parallel wording would look like this:

- Capital punishment is not a deterrent.
- Capital punishment is not constitutional.
- Capital punishment is not civilized.

■ ***Include at least one piece of strong evidence to support each claim.*** Unsupported assertions are unacceptable in an academic debate. If you have subpoints, then you will need to provide evidence for each subpoint. Essentially, your subpoints are the supporting claims for the stock issue stated in the contention. Thus, using evidence and analysis to prove the subpoints is sufficient to support the contention. If the evidence is brief and time permits, you may want to include different types of evidence for some of your arguments. Whatever evidence you do not use in the first speech may be used later in the debate as additional support for your contentions.

CONSTRUCTING CASES ON VALUE PROPOSITIONS

The basic guidelines for constructing a convincing case include creating an introduction and conclusion, and writing and supporting contentions.

In Chapter 5, we noted that a proposition of value asserts the relative worth of something. The word "worth" may not actually appear in the proposition, but some value term does, such as "more important" or "better." One of the stock issues involved in debating propositions of value is that the truth of the proposition depends upon some acceptable standard of judgment, or criteria. First we will discuss the development of an affirmative case and then the development of a negative case on propositions of value.

Advocating Propositions of Value

Constructing a case for value advocacy requires three steps: (1) identify and define a value, (2) place the value in a particular value hierarchy, and (3) select criteria to use in judging the value against the standards of the value hierarchy. We will illustrate these steps with the following example of a value proposition: *Illegal immigration into the U.S. is seriously detrimental to the United States.*

Define the value term. Value debates often focus on defining and defending a key value commonly referred to as a **core value,** which becomes the standard of judgment in debating a value proposition. The core value is the standard argued to be of greatest importance when trying to decide the truth of the value judgment. Since you are trying to advocate your side of the proposition, you need to select a core value that you think most people would accept and one that only your side of the proposition upholds. In our example that *illegal immigration into the U.S. is seriously detrimental to the United States,* what would be the core values of this resolution? Upholding the value of social order, the importance of enforcing laws in a society, stability, and safety would all be reasonable core values related to this topic. If you are opposing the proposition, you might argue that individual freedom and opportunity are the key values that should be defended. As the advocate, you would need to select one of these and prepare to explain why it is the most important value, and that leads to the second step of constructing a case, placing the value in a particular hierarchy to determine its priority and importance.

Identify the value hierarchy. **A value hierarchy** shows the relative importance of different values, how they "stack up" against each other. This is the critical process of explaining and defending why the value advocated by one side takes precedence over all other possible values implicit in the proposition. For example, the right to life and survival is the most basic value for all humans. Without life, there can be no other values. As the advocate, you might also want to offer the testimony of "admirable individuals" who support valuing the object of the proposition this way. For example, Abram Maslow put life-sustaining needs as the most basic, and these needs must come before self-esteem (see Chapter 1). Return to the proposition that *"illegal immigration is seriously detrimental to the U.S."* As the advocate, you have selected the value of social order as your core value. In the affirmative case, you would want to explain how that value is critical to society's survival and ultimately, the continuation of the individual rights and liberty we all cherish. For example, stability and social order through society's enforcement of laws is absolutely essential to the survival of society. Therefore, social order is of greater importance than individual rights. Social order is then necessary and must come first if liberty is to exist and be meaningful. By doing this, the advocate has provided a value hierarchy for making a judgment that will be critical to evaluating the value proposition and determining the outcome of the debate.

Specify the value criteria. The final step in preparing an affirmative case for a proposition of value is to specify the value criteria or criterion. Appropriate value criteria will depend upon the core value selected such as justice, or public safety. Value criteria might include fairness, or public welfare. For example, enforcement of laws may be the test for justice and safety may be important for measuring public welfare. On the illegal immigration proposition, a case upholding the proposition could argue that immigration laws are justified so that society's resources are not overburdened, therefore promoting public safety (the value criterion), which is necessary for gaining societal welfare (the core value). Likewise, enforcement of such laws is a prerequisite for fairness (the value criterion), and fair treatment under the law is necessary for justice (the core value).

Opposing Propositions of Value

When opposing a proposition of value, the negative side in the debate has the burden of rejoinder, meaning it must prove the proposition is false or unreasonable, after the advocate presents a *prima facie* case. To construct the negative case, the opponent uses the same three steps the advocate uses to construct the affirmative case. These steps are to (1) identify and define a value, (2) place the value in a particular value hierarchy, and (3) select criteria to use in judging the value against the standards of the value hierarchy. As we did above, we will develop a negative case on the value proposition that *"illegal immigration into the U.S. is seriously detrimental to the United States."*

Define the value and place it in a value hierarchy. Since the first step for the advocacy was to define terms and to identify a core value, it will be important for the opposing team to present a value that is embraced by rejecting the resolution. Since the focus is on values and their priority within a hierarchy, rarely is it necessary for opponents to argue topicality as they might in policy debates. Instead, the negative case will present a value that accomplishes one of the following: (1) the value can be proven to be superior to the affirmative's value, (2) the negative's value subsumes the opposing value or, (3) the negative agrees with the affirmative's value, but is more likely to achieve the same value by opposing the resolution.

Specify the value criteria. Just as the affirmative case needs to present criteria in support of their value, so must the negative side. Value criteria are the measures by which the facts of the value proposition are said to uphold the core value. If we take the example again of illegal immigration, proving the proposition is detrimental to the United States will require thinking from the opposite perspective. It will require arguing that freedom, autonomy, and the right to a better life, are core values. Appropriate value criteria will once again depend upon the core value selected. Freedom from arbitrary laws may be an important value criterion for liberty or autonomy. Increased access to opportunities (value criterion) may be fundamental to obtaining the right to a better life (core value). The case for rejection of the value proposition regarding illegal immigration will argue that the enforcement of immigration laws deny liberty, autonomy or the right to a better life (core values) because they restrict freedom and deny access to better opportunities for individuals less fortunate than Americans (value criteria).

CONSTRUCTING CASES ON POLICY PROPOSITIONS

Most academic debates involve propositions of policy, and most of you will be debating propositions of policy in your class. As you remember from Chapter 5, a proposition of policy asserts that something should be done; it advocates a course of action. One easy method for identifying a proposition of policy is that the word "should" or "ought" will be stated in the proposition (e.g., The federal government *should* substantially change its foreign policy toward Korea).

Policy debates always include arguments based on claims of fact and/or value since it is necessary to establish relevant facts and prioritize values before reaching decisions about policies. For example, to debate the proposition that the *United States should significantly decrease its troops and military support in Iraq,* requires advocates and opponents to examine the facts and values leading to the war in Iraq. Did Iraq possess weapons of mass destruction? Did the United States have a moral obligation to send troops to Iraq because of the horrendous human rights violations committed against the Iraqi people? Was Iraq a genuine threat to our national security? These questions involve issues of fact and value that are integral to a policy debate about whether or not the United States should withdraw troops from that country.

In this section, we will first explain a step-by-step procedure for constructing an affirmative case designed to advocate a specific policy. Then we will discuss some strategies a debater can use to construct a negative case opposing a policy proposition.

Constructing an Affirmative Case

These arguments should be organized around three of the four stock issues: (1) there is a significant problem(s) or need for a change, (2) the status quo cannot or will not solve this problem (inherency), and (3) the proposed plan can effectively solve the problem or minimize the problem. These three issues will comprise the body of the affirmative case. The stock issue of cost is an issue that opponents of the proposition include in their negative case. We discuss this later in the section on constructing the negative case.

Development of the three stock issues for the advocate comprises the body of the case. Each individual stock issue becomes one or more contentions in the case (i.e., *interdependent* arguments for the proposition). The organizational structure of the speech will vary depending upon which type of affirmative case you choose. There are four types of affirmative cases from which to select: (1) need–plan case, (2) comparative advantages case, (3) goals case, and (4) criteria case. Each of these cases involves the same stock issues (significance, inherency, workability) outlined earlier. The main differences are the order in which the stock issues are presented and the extent to which they are emphasized.

The **need-plan case** is the same as a problem–solution outline: The advocate identifies a significant problem, indicates why the status quo cannot or will not solve the problem, and proposes a workable solution. Below is an outline of this case:

I. There are significant problems/harms in the status quo.
   A. The problem exists.
   B. The problem is significant (severity and scope of problem.)
II. The status quo is unable to eliminate the problem.
   A. Some structural barrier (e.g., law) prevents a solution.
   B. Some motivational barrier (e.g., profit motive) prevents a solution.
III. Presentation of the affirmative plan.
   A. Mandate what the plan will do (i.e., establish a program, pass a law, repeal a current law).
   B. Enforcement (what agent will enforce the plan and how).
   C. Funding (how and who will pay for the plan—if there is a cost to the proposal).
IV. The affirmative plan eliminates or reduces the problem.

Example of a Need-Plan Case

Proposition: *The federal government should significantly strengthen the regulation of mass media communication in the United States*

I. Advertising aimed at children is pervasive.
   A. 8.5 minutes of advertising is shown every hour on Saturday morning.
   B. A child is exposed to 21,000 commercials each year.
II. TV advertising has detrimental effects on young children.
   A. TV ads teach unhealthy consumption patterns to children.
   B. TV ads encourage unnecessary expenditures.
III. The status quo cannot solve the problem.
   A. The FTC does not regulate children's advertising.
   B. Advertising companies will not voluntarily regulate advertising to children.
IV. The affirmative plan
   A. Independent Agency under the Department of Health and Human Services will administer plan:
      1. Eliminate all TV ads directed to audiences comprised of 20% children.
      2. Replace ads with information about nutritional foods and healthy eating.
   B. Funding from general revenue sources
   C. Anyone disobeying this proposal will be subject to fines and/or imprisonment.
V. The affirmative plan saves the American youth from the harms of TV advertising.
   A. A ban on advertising during peak children viewing times will reduce exposure to these messages.
   B. Counter advertising related to nutritional foods will change poor food consumptions patterns among children.

The **comparative advantage case** is an organizational structure demonstrating that the affirmative plan achieves an improvement over the status quo. The advocates are not claiming to solve the entire problem—only that they have a better, more advantageous policy than that of the status quo. In this type of case, the solution (plan) is presented first and its effects (the advantages) are presented afterward. This type of affirmative case must show that the advantages are significant (corresponding to the requirement that a problem be significant in the need-plan case). The advantages must be unique to the plan (corresponding to the requirement that a need be inherent in the need-plan). In other words, nothing short of the affirmative plan can bring about the same advantages. An outline of a comparative advantages case would look like this:

I. Presentation of the affirmative plan
   A. Mandates
   B. Funding
   C. Enforcement
II. The affirmative plan produces the following advantage:
   A. The advantage is significant
   B. The advantage is unique to the affirmative proposal
      1. Certain structural barriers exist (law or the absence of a law)
      2. Current motivational barriers prevent the advantage
   C. The affirmative plan gains the advantage

Example of a Comparative Advantages Case

Proposition: *The federal government should guarantee comprehensive medical care for all citizens in the United States.*

I. Plan: Administered through the Department of Health and Human Services:
   A. U.S. citizens will be guaranteed medical care (free of charge).
   B. All doctors must practice under this plan.
   C. Funding: from a 10% tax increase on all corporations and businesses.
   D. Enforcement: violations are punishable by loss of license, fines, imprisonment.
II. The Affirmative plan will increase access to health care in America.
   A. Access to medical care is denied to millions of people.
   B. The Federal Government has no program that guarantees medical care.
      1. Cuts in funding of Medicaid
      2. States have no health insurance programs for the poor.
      3. Most companies no longer offer affordable medical insurance.
   C. The Affirmative plan guarantees comprehensive medical care.
      1. Everyone will receive free health care.
      2. Doctors must work in this government plan.
      3. The federal government has the financial ability.
III. The Affirmative plan will stop needless death and suffering.
   A. Millions suffer and die from not receiving timely medical care.
   B. Millions of Americans have no way to pay for necessary health insurance.
   C. Employers are not required to provide health insurance to their employees.
   D. Affirmative plan makes health care free to all citizens.

The **goals case** resembles the comparative advantages case by not highlighting a need for change. However, unlike a comparative advantages approach, which advocates a new plan to provide benefits that the status quo cannot achieve, the goals case advocates a new plan to provide the same benefits that are supposed to be attainable in the status quo, but are, in fact, not.

In using the goals case, the advocate must find, state, and accept the goals that were established by the past or current lawmakers and then argue that these goals would be better met through the proposition. This type of case works well with topics focused on curing social ills or improving laws, where the debate proposition endorses the philosophical basis for existing government infrastructure. Additionally, if the advocate is having difficulty proving a significant harm, a goals case allows the advocate to claim substantial benefit from just achieving a status quo goal. This can be enough for a prima facie case. An outline for a goals case would look like this:

  I. The status quo is committed to the attainment of a certain goal.
 II. The status quo fails to meet the goal.
III. Presentation of the advocate's plan is made.
 IV. The plan better meets the status quo's goal.

Example of a Goals Case

Proposition: *The U.S. should significantly change its domestic agricultural policy*

  I. The goal of present agricultural price supports is to help farmers remain financially solvent.
    A. The goal is expressed in laws.
    B. The goal reflects the value of supporting rural ways of life.
 II. The present price support policies preclude achieving this goal
    A. Subsides go primarily to large farms.
    B. Debt collection on small/medium farms is still without relief.
    C. Banks will not allow farmers to refinance loans at lower interest rates.
III. The Plan
    A. Redirect farm subsidy payments to small/medium farms.
    B. Federal Government will underwrite bank loans to small/medium farmers at low interest rates (1% above the prime-rate).
    C. Funding will be through general revenues.
    D. Enforcement includes fines and/or imprisonment.
 IV. This plan is the best means of meeting the goal.
    A. Large-scale farming does not need price supports.
    B. Small/medium-scale farming does need price supports.
    C. Low interest loans will allow farmers to keep from losing their farms.
    D. Small/medium-scale farming is ecologically wise.

Rather than focusing on a particular policy or the reason for a particular policy, the **criteria case** focuses on the characteristics or criteria upon which policy alternatives should be based. This strategy highlights the requirements of an ideal policy and then constructs a plan that meets those standards. If the opponent does not reject those standards (criteria), the advocate can justify a major change in policy direction. The rationale is simple: The advocate's plan should be adopted because it is better able to meet the desired criteria for an effective policy than is the status quo. An outline for a criteria case would look like this:

  I. An optimal policy should meet certain standards/criteria.
 II. The status quo's policy does not meet these standards/criteria.
III. Presentation of the plan
 IV. The advocate's plan meets these standards/criteria.

Example of a Criteria Case

Proposition: *The U.S. should significantly change its energy policy*

   I. A sound energy policy should meet the following criteria:
      A. Energy sources should be abundant.
      B. Energy sources should be cheap.
      C. Energy sources should be eco-friendly.
  II. The current energy policy fails to meet these criteria:
      A. The United States is dependent on fossil fuels and foreign oil imports.
      B. A policy of fossil fuel use and oil imports fails to meet these criteria.
         1. Fossil fuels are finite and limited.
         2. Fossil fuels are imported and expensive.
         3. Fossil fuels damage the environment.
 III. Affirmative plan
      A. Mandate a 10-year phase-out of the use of fossil fuels.
      B. Require a 10% per-year increase over the next 10 years of alternative energy sources, specifically solar power.
      C. Funding: 25% increase corporate taxes on oil companies
      D. Enforcement: By any and all means necessary, including significant fines and/or imprisonment
  IV. Use of Solar power is the optimal energy policy
      A Solar power is abundant.
      B. Solar power is inexpensive.
      C. Solar power is environmentally clean.

Constructing a Negative Case

In any policy debate, the opponent has a single burden: to dispute the affirmative case (including the plan). The advocate has the burden of proof similar to a court of law where the prosecution must prove that an individual is guilty of committing a crime. A defendant only needs to create reasonable doubt of his or her guilt in the minds of the jury in order to be acquitted. Just like a courtroom defense, the opponent does not have to win every argument or every issue in a debate, but only needs to demonstrate that the affirmative case does not met the burden of proof. This is the benefit of *presumption* that we discussed in Chapter 5. In addition to presumption, the negative case against a policy proposition consists of the following:

The negative case includes direct attacks on the affirmative's case. This strategy responds to the affirmative case, point by point, arguing that the reasons for change are wrong or lack proof. Thus, for every claim in the affirmative case, the negative offers a counterclaim asserting that what the affirmative says is false or unimportant. In dealing with specific affirmative contentions, the negative side has several options:

■ Argue that there is no problem. While this may be the most obvious counterclaim in a negative case, it is often difficult to defend because the affirmative will likely have a legitimate claim of harm or have identified a problem that exists in the status quo.

■ Argue that the problem exists but it is not significant. The opponent attempts in some way to minimize the impact of the problem. For example, the opponent can argue that there is no widespread harm. Perhaps the examples in the affirmative case are atypical and isolated, but are not national in scope. Another argument is that the problem is less important (see discussion above on *value hierarchy)* than the problems caused by the affirmative plan (see *disadvantages* below).

- Claim that the problem or advantage is not inherent; that the status quo can achieve the same results as the affirmative plan. This approach is referred to as ***defense of the status quo***. The aim is to show that the status quo is dynamic and ever changing and is fully capable of dealing with the problem outlined by the affirmative. You could argue that there are several laws on the books, including state and local regulations that can solve the problem in combination with federal laws. It is possible that some legislation has just been implemented and needs time to see if it will be effective. Therefore, rushing to adopt a new proposal is unwarranted until the current laws have an opportunity to be successful. It is also possible that there are private programs that reduce the need for federal action. We may not need national health care if privately run free medical clinics can solve the problem.

- Offer a **minor repair** to the status quo. A minor repair is an alteration of the status quo that is as effective as the affirmative plan, but involves substantially less change than that proposed by the advocate. In this line of argument, the negative case concedes that the status quo is flawed in some way, but demonstrates that the current system has the necessary laws on the books or agencies in place; what is lacking is consistent enforcement, extensive funding, or necessary personnel. For example, an affirmative case might contend that there should be harsher penalties against drunk driving. The opponent could respond that strict penalties already exist and that enforcement needs to be strengthened in some way.

The negative case includes the option to offer a counter plan. A **counter plan** is the opponent's plan for dealing with the problem or providing the advantage identified in the affirmative case. When presenting a counter plan, the opponent admits there is a need to change the status quo but claims there is a better way than the affirmative plan. Proposing a counter plan may be a good idea, but the opponent in a policy debate must make sure that the counter plan meets the following three requirements:

1. ***The counter plan must be nontopical.*** The explanation for this is quite simple and straightforward: If the negative case advocates a *topical* (propositional) plan, it is not opposing the proposition. On the other hand, if an affirmative case advocates a *nontopical* (nonpropositional) plan, it is not supporting the proposition. Therefore, the opponent should explain that the counter plan is different from the policy proposition. A good example of this would be on a policy proposition that requires a manufacturer to make safer products. The affirmative case might argue that all cars should be equipped with airbags. The opponent's counter plan could be a law requiring individuals to wear seat belts, instead of equipping automobiles with airbags. Since cars are already manufactured with seat belts, it is not the manufacturer who is making the cars safer, but the consumer who is buckling up. The counter plan differs from the proposition since it doesn't require the manufacturer to make a safer product.

2. ***A counter plan must be competitive—not*** able to "co-exist" with the affirmative plan. This means that for the counter plan to constitute a reason to oppose the proposition, we must be forced to choose between the proposition (affirmative plan) and the counter plan. In other words, the plans must be *mutually exclusive.* Otherwise, why not adopt both plans? For example, if an affirmative plan imposed a ban on weapons sales to Middle Eastern countries, a competitive counter plan could increase weapons sales to these countries because the two

plans are mutually exclusive—one cannot both ban weapon sales and increase sales to the same countries simultaneously.

3. *A counter plan must be superior to the affirmative plan.* The counter plan must be more beneficial than the affirmative plan: save more lives, solve more of the problems, or avoid certain "costs" or disadvantages. Opponents to the proposition usually do this by proving that the affirmative's plan produces more disadvantages than the negative's plan. For example, the requirement for all cars manufactured in the United States be equipped with airbags is going to cost a great deal of money, which will be passed on to the consumer in the form of higher prices for cars. Since seat belts are already in the cars and cost very little, it would be cheaper to have mandatory seat belt laws than to require cars to be equipped with airbags.

The negative case includes attacks on the affirmative's plan. Attacks on an affirmative plan consist of workability arguments and disadvantages. A workability argument says that the affirmative plan will not solve the problem or provide the advantage noted in the affirmative case (workability issue). A disadvantage argument is that the affirmative's plan will produce harmful consequences.

Although an affirmative plan may look good on paper, it might be unworkable in practice. Consider mandatory seat belt laws mentioned above. There is no doubt that seat belts can save many lives. However, it is very difficult to enforce such laws since it is practically impossible to spot every driver who is not wearing a seat belt. The shortage of police in many local communities would make enforcement of these laws unlikely.

The negative takes the position that the affirmative plan is flawed and will not work. Simply put, there is something structurally wrong with the plan. Possible defects could include poor administration, lack of adequate funding, staff, or technology. For instance, the reason the problem of storing nuclear waste material exists is because the underground containers designed to store the toxins eventually leak. Despite the best intentions of the affirmative, until better storage containers are developed, nuclear waste will still harm individuals with or without the affirmative plan. Thus, the affirmative plan should be rejected because it is unworkable due to limited technology.

The affirmative plan may not meet the need or accrue the advantages claimed. The negative takes the position that even if the plan worked, it would not accomplish its purpose, which is to say it will not solve the problem it is supposed to solve. The argument is that other causes exist for the problems noted in the status quo instead of, or in addition to, the causes identified in the affirmative case. As a result, the plan will be hampered by those factors, and the advantages will not be gained or the problem will not be solved. For example, the affirmative might argue that individuals without medical insurance do not visit a doctor because they cannot afford to pay for the services. The affirmative plan guarantees free medical care. The opponent could argue that there are many reasons besides cost that people don't seek medical help: they don't have time, they fear doctors, they don't feel sick, they don't live near medical clinics. All these are reasons many people won't seek treatment regardless of the cost. Thus, the affirmative plan cannot guarantee its advantages or guarantee solving the problem.

Disadvantages are the "costs" or harmful consequences of the affirmative plan. Even though the plan may work and solve the problem that the affirmative identifies, implementation of the plan may have undesirable side effects that warrant its rejection. Disadvantages comprise the fourth stock issue in policy debate (i.e., the cost issue). All disadvantages contain the following three components:

1. *A disadvantage must be caused by the affirmative plan.* The negative must identify how the plan causes the disadvantages. Does the plan trigger additional spending? Does it cause

inflation? In some cases, the link to the case will be obvious, but in other instances, the negative must provide evidence to support its link.

2. *A disadvantage must be unique to the affirmative plan.* This means that the disadvantage should result only from the affirmative plan. If additional federal spending or economic growth is likely to happen in the status quo, even if the plan is not adopted, the disadvantage cannot be a reason to reject the affirmative plan.

3. *The cost of disadvantages must outweigh the benefit of solving the problem.* There may be several internal links leading from the plan (e.g., using general revenue to pay for the plan) to the impact of cutting programs in welfare to the individuals harmed by these cuts (see sample disadvantage below).

A Sample Negative Disadvantage

I. The affirmative will spend billions of dollars to implement the plan.
II. Welfare programs will be cut because they lack political support.
　A. Food stamps have traditionally been the target of budget cuts.
　B. Food stamps save thousands from starvation a year.
　C. Medicaid has traditionally been the target of budget cuts.
　D. Medicaid saves millions from disease and suffering.

SUMMARY

This chapter examined how affirmative and negative cases are constructed for both value and policy propositions. In order to construct a case for either side of a proposition, the debater must prepare by analyzing the proposition, defining terms, and recording and organizing evidence. Debating a value proposition requires both sides to identify a core value, value hierarchy, and specify value criteria to be used as a standard for judgment. Debating a policy proposition requires the advocate to present contentions that support with evidence the existence of a significant and inherent problem, and a plan to solve the problem. Several different affirmative cases were explained, including the need-plan, comparative advantages, goal, and criteria cases—all designed to provide a prima facie case for the proposition. The opponent's negative case on a proposition of policy must include direct attacks on the affirmative case, but also includes the use of minor repairs, counter plans, topicality, workability, and disadvantages.

In a debate, the affirmative has the advantage of establishing the framework of the argumentation and defining the issues in the debate while the negative, because of presumption, can be successful by supporting their position on a single issue. In the end, the key to being a successful debater, either on the affirmative or negative side, is the level of preparation, including research, analysis, and case construction the individual is committed to doing prior to the debate.

NOTES

1 A good discussion of brainstorming can be found in http://en.wikipedia.org/wiki/Brainstorming.
2 Rybacki, K..C., & Rybacki, D. J. (2004). *Advocacy and opposition* (pp. 116–118). Boston, MA: Allyn & Bacon.

Chapter 7

Presenting a Convincing Case

CHAPTER OUTLINE

I. Managing Speech Anxiety
  A. Causes and Symptoms of Speech Anxiety
  B. Techniques for Managing Speech Anxiety
II. Delivering the Speech
  A. The Elements of a Good Delivery
  B. Developing a Good Delivery
  C. Structuring an Oral Argument
III. Attacking and Defending Arguments
  A. Taking and Using Notes
  B. Refuting Arguments
IV. Cross-Examining the Opposing Side
V. Summary

KEY TERMS

Burden of Clash
Counterclaim
Constructive Speech
Critical Listening
Cross-Examination
Delivery
Direct Speech
Dynamic Speech
Extending an Argument
Fluent Speech

Flow Sheet
Intelligible Speech
Rebuttal
Refutation
Signposting
Speech Anxiety
Stage Fright
Transition
Unobtrusive Speech

When it comes to the business of persuasion, most of us would like to believe that having the "truth on our side" is all that really matters, that somehow "the facts will speak for themselves." But how we present the facts may be as important as the facts themselves in gaining the acceptance of an audience. A humorous illustration of this point occurs in the movie, *My Cousin Vinny*. The title character, Vinny, played by actor Joe Pesci, is a personal injury attorney living in Brooklyn who agrees to defend his young cousin, Billy, and Billy's friend Stan, both falsely charged with murdering a convenience store clerk in Alabama. With no criminal trial experience, and having just passed his bar exam after five failed attempts, Vinny struts into the courtroom with a sense of confidence that belies his lack of training. Not surprisingly, his ignorance and poor presentation skills immediately get him into trouble with the judge. After appearing at the arraignment in a leather jacket and no tie, failing to enter a plea, and behaving disrespectfully, the judge throws Vinny into jail for contempt of court. In his second appearance in court, Vinny fails to cross-examine any of the witnesses.

Following Vinny's poor performance, Stan decides to use the public defender, but Billy gives Vinny a second chance. Unfortunately, Vinny sleeps through the prosecutor's opening statement. With nothing prepared and no idea what the jury just heard, Vinny makes a brief opening statement of his own: "Everything that guy just said is BS. Thank you." Then Stan's attorney, suffering from a severe case of stage fright, delivers a stupid and stuttering opening statement, and when cross-examining the first prosecution witness, asks questions that actually strengthen the prosecutor's case against Billy and Stan.

Sometimes having the truth on your side is not enough. In addition to knowing "the rules of the game," it helps to master the basic skills of presenting a convincing case, which include: managing speech anxiety, delivering a speech, refuting arguments, taking notes, giving a rebuttal, and cross-examining the opposing side.

MANAGING SPEECH ANXIETY

Stage fright is the mental and physical manifestations of the fear associated with a public performance. The most significant factor is the ***fear of rejection*** by a critical audience. Many people in the "public eye" such as musicians, actors, politicians, and athletes probably experience varying degrees of stage fright from time to time, but have found workable ways of keeping it from hurting their performances. Stage fright leads to an array of symptoms ranging from a little nervous energy to various sensations that can make the performer feel queasy, panicky, forgetful, and lightheaded.

One common type of stage fright, **speech anxiety**, is the specific fear of giving a speech in front of a potentially disapproving audience. What are the causes and symptoms of speech anxiety? And what can you do about it?

Causes and Symptoms of Speech Anxiety

On very rare occasions, the consequences of speech anxiety can become debilitating, making it difficult for someone to deliver a speech. More often, speech anxiety produces only mild symptoms that help rather than hurt a speaker's performance, releasing just enough adrenalin to help a speaker prepare and focus on the task at hand. Still, there are a number of factors that make a difference, contributing to more or less anxiety. These factors include certain characteristics of the audience, as well as attitudes, beliefs, and experiences of the speaker[1]:

- ***The size of the audience.*** In general, people tend to be more anxious about speaking to a large rather than to a small group of people. On the other hand, some people feel more nervous in front of a smaller audience because of the increased "closeness" of smaller audiences compared to larger audiences.
- ***The status of the audience.*** The disapproval of a high-status audience capable of rewarding or punishing a speaker carries greater "weight" (creating more anxiety) than does an audience without such power.
- ***Familiarity with the audience.*** Speaking to a group of strangers creates more anxiety than speaking to friends or acquaintances does.
- ***Prior experiences.*** Having had an unpleasant experience giving a speech can create some fear about giving another speech.

- ***Focusing on the fear.*** Dwelling on the "negatives" such as not being able to remember what to say, or making a bad impression, only add to a speaker's anxiety.
- ***Beliefs about public speaking.*** Certain misconceptions contribute to anxiety such as the belief that reading the speech or not looking at the audience will help, or the belief that the audience can easily tell if a speaker is nervous.
- ***Preparation.*** This factor, more than any other, determines a speaker's level of anxiety: the less prepared a speaker is, the more anxious a speaker will feel.

Overcoming speech anxiety is one of the many challenges of effective public speaking.

The fear of giving a speech produces four kinds of reactions that comprise the symptoms of speech anxiety. The first kind includes various ***fight-or-flight reactions***, our body's natural responses to stress: accelerated heart rate, rapid breathing, perspiration, queasy-feeling stomach, dry mouth, wide eyes, and more.[2] A second kind consists of ***avoidance behaviors***, indicating a speaker's desire to "get it over with," such as avoiding eye contact with the audience, speaking fast, and not getting close to the audience. A third set of reactions are facial, vocal, and bodily ***expressions of fear*** that may be difficult to suppress (e.g., worried brow, shaky or high-pitched voice, nervous mannerisms), as well as all sorts of self-conscious, fear-related thoughts that occur before speaking (e.g., "they are going to be bored with my speech," "I'll never be able to remember what I need to say,") and while speaking (e.g., "they know I'm nervous," "I'm speaking too fast,").

The experience of speech anxiety is a natural and ordinary part of public speaking, and it rarely interferes with a speaker's performance. Still, there are practical steps any speaker can take to keep the anxiety from becoming a problem.

Techniques for Managing Speech Anxiety

As we noted earlier, some degree of speech anxiety is desirable because it gives a speaker increased energy and focus. But in order to prevent the debilitating effects that may result from too much anxiety, we recommend some activities a few days before debating, and others right before or during your debate.

Days before your scheduled debate, adequate preparation is the key. Our best advice: ***prepare your case*** as completely as possible. Most likely, you won't experience unpleasant levels of anxiety if you know what you are going to say and how you are going to say it. You should plan to finish preparing your debate case at least a few days before presenting it. This will give you time to practice, which will lessen your uncertainty about the experience. You'll be more confident if you have a good idea of what you're going to do and say in advance. Even the most experienced speakers mentally rehearse before giving a speech.

Make a concerted effort to ***adopt a positive outlook*** about your upcoming debate. This means believing you have something worthwhile and important to say. It means you recognize how silly it is to dwell on the little things that make you self-conscious and that the audience will not notice anyway. It means you find nothing terrible about being in a situation that naturally increases your adrenalin and your blood pressure. It means you realize how supportive your audience will be—especially since they are "in the same boat" you are in and will identify with your nervousness. It also means you know, even if you feel "butterflies" in your stomach as you stand up to give your speech that they will disappear as soon as you begin to speak. And finally, it means you accept the principle that public speaking does, in fact, build self-confidence. The more you do it, the better you will feel about yourself.

As you wait your turn to speak, **_try one or more relaxation techniques_**, such as deep breathing, to ease your stress. Some public speakers benefit from constructive self-talk or imagery (i.e., saying something to yourself like "my argument is really good" or picturing yourself giving a good speech). In a debate, most speakers get so caught up in the flow of the argument that they have no time to get nervous waiting their turn.

Once you begin speaking, try to **_act confidently_** (even if you are not feeling very confident). If you are nervous, this may require some acting ability at first. But you will find that the more confident you behave, the more confident you feel. A confident demeanor consists of steady eye contact, an assertive tone, fearless facial expressions, forceful gestures, good posture, and the absence of nervous mannerisms (i.e., fidgeting). In short, confident behavior leads to a feeling of confidence, which promotes confident behavior and fewer uncomfortable symptoms of speech anxiety.

DELIVERING THE SPEECH

A confident demeanor, part of what we expect from a good speaker, not only lessens the impact of speech anxiety, but it contributes to the overall success of a speaker as well. Even the most informed and opinionated listeners are not immune to the influence of a speaker's **delivery**—the _nonverbal communication_ of the speaker, including his or her physical appearance, eye contact, posture, positioning, gestures, facial expressions, and tone of voice (everything but the words). A strong delivery adds considerable impact to a speaker's arguments while simultaneously (and often unknowingly) shaping listeners' impressions of the speaker's competence and character. First, we will identify the elements of a good delivery and then we will discuss how to develop a good delivery.

A good speech delivery should be sufficiently clear, indicate knowledge of the topic, express interest in both the audience and the topic, and avoid distracting the audience.

The Elements of a Good Delivery

What are the basic elements of a "good" delivery? Regardless of the circumstances, a good delivery should be sufficiently clear, indicate knowledge of the topic, express interest in both the audience and the topic, and avoid distracting the audience.[3] Because of its heavy focus on the _text_ of an argument (claim, evidence, reasoning), a speaker's delivery may be somewhat less important in an academic debate than it is in other public speaking contexts. However, as we explain below, even the most compelling argument will lose much of its appeal if a speaker presents it in an unconvincing manner.

1. *A good delivery is intelligible.* No matter how strong an argument is on paper, to be an effective *oral* argument, it needs to be heard. If listeners don't "pick up" a speaker's argument because he speaks too softly, too fast, or mumbles too often, the argument has absolutely no chance of succeeding. Probably, the most fundamental "bottom line" quality of a good delivery is **intelligible speech**, speech that is clear and comprehensible.

2. *A good delivery is fluent.* Another important element of a good delivery is **fluent speech**, which is free of extraneous pauses and hesitations—the "ums" and "ahs" we hear so often. Pauses and hesitations are signs of thinking and are more prevalent when a speaker is either unprepared or uninformed, but because they also tend to increase when speakers are self-conscious, listeners sometimes attribute nervousness to speakers who pause and hesitate a lot.

3. *A good delivery is direct.* In Chapter 1, we discussed the importance of using an *extemporaneous* style of speaking, which is a prepared style (in contrast to *impromptu* speaking) that relies on the use of limited notes, such as an outline, and not on memory or manuscript. An extemporaneous speaking style promotes speaker–audience contact in a way that no other speaking style does. Without this quality of **direct speech,** a speaker will have difficulty holding the attention of her audience, and even the strongest argument is likely to fall on deaf ears. More than any other quality, direct speech distinguishes an oral argument from a written argument.

4. *A good delivery is dynamic.* Some speakers seem to have little or no passion for what they are saying. They don't seem to care. A lifeless, monotone voice, a lack of gestures, and an expressionless face contribute to such impressions. In contrast, **dynamic speech**, which is forceful, energetic, and animated, conveys to an audience the impression that a speaker cares deeply about the points she is trying to get across.

5. *A good delivery is unobtrusive.* Ideally, a speaker's delivery carries and supports his message without drawing attention away from it. **Unobtrusive speech** is free of distracting movements, expressions, and sounds, such as shuffling your feet, tapping your fingers, touching your face or hair, pacing back and forth, swaying from side to side, speaking too loud, mispronouncing words, sighing, smiling nervously, and so on. Clothing and accessories too can sometimes be a source of distraction.

Developing a Good Delivery

The basic elements of a good delivery change little from one speaking context to another. That is, a good speaker needs to be intelligible, fluent, direct, dynamic, and unobtrusive in any public speaking situation, though the demands and constraints of one situation may differ from another (e.g., the size of the audience, the opportunity to prepare, the formality of the occasion, the level of surrounding noise, etc.)

Most tips for developing a good delivery represent a broad consensus among experienced speakers, teachers, coaches, and consultants (e.g., make good eye contact, use some pauses and gesture for emphasis, speak up but don't speak too fast, maintain good posture, dress for the occasion, etc.). Listed below are some recommendations that we think are particularly relevant and important in the context of a classroom debate.

Delivery Element	Definition	Recommendations
Intelligible speech	Clear and understandable	■ Project to the back of the room ■ Get feedback from others ■ Audiotape the speech and listen to it
Fluent speech	Free of pauses/hesitations	■ Become knowledgeable on topic ■ Become familiar with your outline ■ Mentally rehearse the speech
Direct speech	Focused on the audience	■ *Follow the four steps of oral argument* ■ Limit amount of text on each card ■ Make eye contact with individuals
Dynamic speech	Forceful and animated	■ Remember it's a public performance ■ Speak with feeling and conviction ■ Practice the speech a few times
Unobtrusive speech	Free of distractions	■ Watch a videotape of your speech ■ Get feedback from others ■ Practice the speech a few times

An academic debate is a unique speaking context, so some of our recommendations, such as "following the four steps of oral argument" require elaboration. We discuss this specific technique in the next section on structuring an oral argument. Other recommendations, such as make eye contact, know your topic, practice, get feedback, and watch a video of your speech are straightforward and useful ways of improving your delivery in any public speaking situation.

Structuring an Oral Argument

An oral argument differs from a written argument in several important ways, especially in the context of an academic debate. Aside from the need to have a good delivery, a speaker needs to present arguments in a way that allows and facilitates extensive *note taking* by all of the participants—judges and other debaters. As a student taking notes in your classes, you know how important it is for an instructor to be clear, well organized, and even a bit redundant, so it's easy for you and all the other students in the class to take notes. In this sense, an academic debate creates a similar challenge for speakers and note-takers. But the exclusive focus on presenting, attacking, and defending arguments makes debate participation a much different sort of challenge.

The most widely used method of structuring an oral argument in an academic debate is known as *the 4-step method.* Using this method correctly lets the speaker communicate arguments efficiently and persuasively, while also making it relatively easy for everyone to take good notes. And as we will see shortly, taking good notes is an indispensable part of debating (see section below on attacking and defending arguments).

Use the following four steps each time you present an argument backed up by some type of evidence (e.g., facts, statistics, testimony, etc.):

STEP 1: State the claim. The first thing you do is tell us clearly and concisely the claim in the argument you are going to try and prove. For the sake of accuracy and time, you should read your claim from your notes. If your claims are "wordy" and rambling, they will be time-consuming and difficult to write down. Save any elaboration for the next step. Also, be sure to signpost each of your claims. **Signposting** lets your listeners know that you are introducing another claim. The simplest and clearest way to "announce" a claim is to use the same number or letter you use in your case outline. You need a slight modification in this step when attacking rather than presenting an argument: State the other side's claim and then present your opposing claim.

STEP 2: Sell the claim. After you state your claim, you need to "sell" it to your audience. In an academic debate, the audience includes one or more "judges" who decide the winner and loser of the debate (more on this in Chapter 8). Selling the claim may involve saying what it means. More importantly, it requires you to convince the judges that your claim strongly supports your position on a *stock issue*. As we discussed in Chapters 5 and 6, issues determine the outcome of a debate. Part of selling a claim is also connecting with your audience. Therefore, you should *make eye contact* during this step and avoid reading from your notes, as you did when merely stating your claim (step 1).

STEP 3: Support the claim. When you finish selling your claim by making eye contact with your audience, saying what the claim means (if necessary), and explaining how your claim advances your position on an issue, you need to support the claim with *evidence*. To do this, read an evidence card or read the evidence from your speech outline. Be sure to state the *source* of the evidence before reading the evidence (e.g., examples, statistics, etc.). Do not try to present your evidence from memory; you risk getting it wrong, which can prove embarrassing later.

STEP 4: Summarize the claim. The final step is to briefly review your argument, emphasizing its importance to your case. At a minimum, you must restate the claim, which serves as a **transition** to your next argument. Transitions are a vital part of any speech, providing a "bridge" from one point to the next. This step also gives the other participants a second chance to check their notes and make sure they recorded the argument correctly.

ATTACKING AND DEFENDING ARGUMENTS

Debate is a turn-taking activity. Each side gets an opportunity to make their case and to dispute the case of the other side. While there are different formats for structuring academic debates, all of the formats adhere to a strictly enforced set of rules about when each side speaks and how long each side can speak (see Chapter 8). Another feature of academic debate is the obligation of each side to respond directly to the arguments of the other side. This **burden of clash** forces debaters to record their own arguments and those of the other side. One of the caveats in academic debate is that "silence means consent." In other words, if you fail to respond to an opposing argument, you are de-facto agreeing with that argument.

Taking and Using Notes

Taking notes in a debate is a vital and complex skill; it requires an ability to listen carefully and continuously, to distinguish between important and unimportant arguments, and to record arguments and evidence in a speedy but accurate manner. Debaters take notes using a **flow sheet**, which is a sheet of paper divided into columns, with each column showing the arguments presented in a particular speech. Debaters refer to note-taking as "flowing" the debate. Debate speeches consist of constructive speeches and rebuttals. A **constructive speech** presents the affirmative or negative case. A **rebuttal** gives each side an opportunity to extend the arguments presented in constructive speeches. **Extending an argument** means responding directly to the argument of a previous speaker in a way that advances debate on that argument.

The sample flow sheet on the following page shows a brief three-speech debate on the topic of illegal immigration (two constructive speeches and a single rebuttal). The first column shows an affirmative case advocating a policy to tighten border security against illegal immigration. The second column shows the opponent's specific responses to the affirmative case as well as the negative's own prepared case against the proposition, which in this case consists of three disadvantages of adopting the affirmative plan (the cost issue). When the negative case includes arguments not addressed in the affirmative case, such as disadvantages, debaters refer to these arguments as *off-case arguments*. Finally, the third column, the affirmative rebuttal, shows the affirmative responses to the negative attacks against the affirmative case, and the affirmative responses to the negative case (i.e., the disadvantages).

Sample Flow Sheet of a Debate Consisting of Three Speeches**

Affirmative Case	Negative Case	Affirmative Rebuttal
I. *Illegal immigration harmful* • *damages public services* • *Rep. Lee quote* • *Overcrowded schools in CA* • *increases crime rate* • *endangers national security*	• *lower prices helps all* • *BLS study* • *biased source* • *more examples needed* • *they fill jobs no one wants* • *Sen. Hale quote* • *business saves $* • *UPA survey* • *???* • *improve law enforcement*	• *public loses tax $* • *Rep. Jones agrees* • *schools in New Mexico* • *Senator is corporate ally* • *public services suffer* • *increased crime* • *beneficial to secure borders*
II. *Current laws ineffective* • *employers keep hiring* • *desire to flee country* • *insecure borders*	• *plan won't solve* • *terrorists get passports* • *punish employers* • *helps economy*	• *not either-or; can do both* • *public services hurt more*

III. *Plan can lessen problem*
• *resources available*
• *decreases entry into United States*
• *secures the border*
	• *not an increase*
	• *border patrol OK now*
	• *plan won't work*
	• *will raise taxes or cut social programs*
	• *fences don't stop them*
	• *fences don't stop*
	  1. *hurt poor countries*
	  2. *hurt businesses*
	  3. *divert tax $*
		• *so what?*
		• *not enough*
		• *not necessary*
		• *with more border patrol*
		• *we can continue aiding*
		• *only in the short-run*
		• *free market will solve*
		• *not necessary*

_____
**Cited evidence shown only for constructive speeches on the first contention.

Refuting Arguments

Attacking and defending arguments requires strong critical listening skills and a well-organized system of finding and using evidence. One of the most important challenges in debate is **refutation**, the act of "refuting" or disproving an opposing argument. Taking good notes is necessary but not sufficient. So, how do you refute an opposing argument? By studying our sample flow sheet, you can see that debaters try to flow (record) arguments across the columns by aligning affirmative and negative claims where they represent points of disagreement, where affirmative and negative arguments **clash**. Debaters use these flow sheets for **point-by-point refutation** against the other side (i.e., refuting each opposing point, one after another, from the top of the column to the bottom). As we noted earlier, the *burden of clash* in a debate makes it necessary to *extend arguments*, not merely repeat them. Of course, an exception occurs when the other side fails to respond. For example, on our sample flow sheet, the question marks (???) indicate that the opponent (negative) did not respond to the affirmative case argument on crime resulting from illegal immigration Thus, it would be permissible for the advocate to repeat this argument in the rebuttal, adding only that the opponent apparently agrees with this point.

In Chapter 2, we analyzed the parts of an argument. You may recall that the basic building blocks of any argument are the claim, the grounds (evidence supporting the claim), and the warrant (the reasoning in the argument). Thus, there are three ways to refute an opposing argument: (1) defend a counterclaim; (2) attack the evidence supporting the claim; and/or (3) attack the reasoning in the argument.

To illustrate these three ways of refuting an argument, we will use an affirmative case contention on the harms of illegal immigration shown on our sample flow sheet: damage to public services (the first subpoint under the first contention). The advocate claims that illegal immigration is overcrowding the public school system:

Claim: *Illegal immigration is overcrowding the public schools*

Evidence: *Illegal immigration in California is overcrowding the public schools*

Reasoning: *California is a representative example of how illegal immigration is affecting public schools in the United States*

One way to refute an argument is to defend (support) a **counterclaim**, which contradicts the opposing claim. Therefore, you could argue that illegal immigration is *not* overcrowding the public schools. Of course, you would need some type of evidence, such as statistics or testimony, to back up your counterclaim. Another way to refute an opposing argument is to point out some weakness in the evidence supporting the claim. In the above argument, you might question the objectivity of the source or the validity of the study alleging that California schools are overcrowded and illegal immigration is to blame. A final way to refute an opposing argument is to identify some flaw in the argument's reasoning. For instance, the claim above depends on a single example—that of California. Any *generalization* based on a single case is always tentative at best. What is happening in California's schools may not be happening elsewhere.

CROSS-EXAMINING THE OPPOSING SIDE

Most academic debates permit limited interaction between opposing sides, which takes place during a brief **cross-examination** period (see Chapter 8). Borrowing from the courtroom model, academic debates give debaters an opportunity to *question* the other side as a way of weakening opposing arguments and strengthening their own.

During the cross-examination period, one debater assumes the role of questioner and the other debater becomes a respondent. The questioner must only ask questions and not make statements and the respondent should not ask questions. The goal of the questioner is to take control of the cross-examination period and try to weaken the respondent's case and advance his or her own case. The goal of the respondent is to avoid losing any ground in the debate, without being uncooperative or evasive. Since we expect the questioner to take charge, our focus here is on what the questioner should try to accomplish.

Borrowing from the courtroom model, academic debates give speakers an opportunity to question the other side as a way of weakening opposing arguments and strengthening their own.

1. ***Analyze an opposing argument.*** Although the primary objective is to advance your position in the debate, you may need information from the respondent in order to analyze an argument—to identify the claim, the evidence, and the reasoning. In this regard, there are many reasons why you may need information from the respondent: you did not hear something such as the date of the evidence; you want to check the accuracy of your notes; you do not understand the reasoning in an argument; you are unsure about the wording of a contention or a subpoint. Of course, while it is a good idea to pursue this objective, spending too much time clarifying the respondent's case does little to advance your position in the debate, unless the information you obtain enables you to expose a weakness in the respondent's case or strengthen your own.

2. ***Expose a weakness in the other side's case.*** A more productive way to use the cross-examination period is to point out any flaws you notice in the respondent's arguments such as a lack of evidence or a fallacy in reasoning. Here are some examples of questions intended to accomplish this objective:

   a. *"You based your contention on a study that was done 15 years ago. Do you have any evidence that is not out-dated?"*

   b. *"You said that a similar program has failed in other states, but you didn't present any evidence to support this claim, correct?"*

   c. *"Who did you quote to support this point? Do you have any unbiased sources to back up this point?"*

   d. *"Do you have any other examples of where this has occurred?"*

   e. *"Are you saying that if we adopt this plan, then the next thing you know it, millions of people will die? Isn't this a slippery slope fallacy?"*

   When asking questions intended to expose a weakness in the other side's case, there is a well-known principle governing the conduct of cross-examination: never ask a question to which you do not know the answer. In other words, be sure the answer to your question will in fact expose a weakness and not strength in the respondent's case.

3. ***Set up an argument.*** As we noted earlier, one way to refute an opposing argument is to defend a counterclaim. To that end, you may use all or part of the cross-examination period to introduce and support one or more claims. Of course, you must ask questions that accomplish this objective. The most direct way is to ask the respondent if he or she is aware of something. This "did you know" technique lets you present evidence supporting one of your claims

(e.g., "did you know that gasoline prices have dropped 8% this past month?"). But an indirect, and more effective way is to use a line of questioning that sets up the entire argument, as in the sample cross-examination on gun control (shown below), in which the questioner sets up the argument that laws making it more difficult to purchase handguns may only increase the purchases of long guns, which are more dangerous than handguns.[4]

Sample Cross-Examination to Set Up an Argument*

1. **Q:** "You claim that many people are killed or seriously injured by handguns during crimes. Is that correct?"
2. **A:** "Yes, in fact I read two pieces of evidence on that point."
3. **Q:** "Well, didn't people commit crimes before the advent of handguns?"
4. **A:** "Of course. But . . ."
5. **Q:** "If your plan went into effect, wouldn't people still commit crimes?"
6. **A:** "Yes, but they wouldn't be shooting people."
7. **Q:** "Your plan only makes it harder for people to get handguns, right? I mean, it doesn't regulate long guns, does it?"
8. **A:** "Handguns are used a lot more often by criminals than long guns are."
9. **Q:** "And that's because handguns are so easy to purchase, right? I mean that's why you want to make them harder to purchase, correct?"
10. **A:** "Yes."
11. **Q:** "And your plan makes it a lot harder for people to get guns, handguns?"
12. **A:** "A lot harder."
13. **Q:** "So doesn't it make sense to assume that people who want to commit crimes will purchase long guns instead of handguns?"
14. **A:** "They might."
15. **Q:** "Isn't it true that someone who is shot by a long gun is more likely to be seriously injured or killed than someone who is shot by a handgun?"
16. **A:** "I don't know, maybe."

---

*Pages 225–226 From *Critical Thinking Through Debate* by Joseph Corcoran et al. Copyright © 2000 by Kendall/Hunt Publishing Co. Reprinted with permission

SUMMARY

The ability to present a convincing case for or against a proposition may require some effort to minimize the symptoms of speech anxiety resulting from self-consciousness and a fear of audience disapproval. Techniques for managing anxiety include preparation, adopting a positive outlook, relaxation techniques, and acting in a confident manner.

An effective presentation also requires a strong delivery consisting of intelligible, fluent, direct, dynamic, and unobtrusive speech. An oral argument differs from a written one, especially when listeners need accurate and comprehensive notes. For this reason, we recommend the 4-step method of stating, selling, supporting, and summarizing claims.

Debates involve the clash of opposing arguments, recorded on flow sheets that debaters use to refute opposing arguments, which includes defending a counterclaim, attacking evidence, and/or attacking the reasoning in an argument. Debaters also use cross-examination, which gives them an opportunity to analyze and weaken opposing arguments and to set up their own arguments.

NOTES

1 Hoff, N., Remland, M., Warnemunde, D., & Ross, R. (1986). *The basics of public speaking*. Dubuque, IA: Kendall Hunt.

2 A good discussion of this appears in http://changingminds.org/explanations/brain/fight_flight.htm.

3 Hoff, Remland, Warnemunde, & Ross. (1986).

4 This sample cross-examination appears in Corcoran, J. M., Nelson, M., & Perella, J. (2006). *Critical thinking through debate* (pp. 225–226). Dubuque, IA: Kendall Hunt.

Chapter 8

Argumentation and Debate in Different Educational Formats

CHAPTER OUTLINE

KEY TERMS

Academic Debate
American Forensics Association
Applied Debate
CEDA
Contract Debates
Disputations
Judging Paradigm
Lay Judges
Lincoln-Douglas Debate

National Forensics Association
NDT
Parliamentary Debate
Policymaker Judge
Point of Order
Point of Information
Skills Judge
Stock Issues Judge

There are two broad categories of debate: applied and academic. **Applied debate** addresses propositions in which the advocates have a special interest, and the debate takes place before a judge or an audience with the power to render a binding decision.[1] In Chapter 9, we will explore the various professional contexts for applied debates, such as judicial and political settings. The second category, **academic debate,** is an invention of educational institutions and provides learning opportunities for students. In this chapter, we discuss the numerous educational debate formats currently available for college students. However, in order to appreciate the evolution of contemporary debate practices, it is important to understand the rich heritage of intercollegiate debate.

ORIGINS OF ACADEMIC DEBATE

Academic debate began at least 2,400 years ago when the scholar Protagoras (481–411 B.C.), called the "Father of Debate," conducted debates among his students in Athens. He created themes in which he required his pupils to argue the pros and cons as a practical exercise to train them to participate in Greek society.[2] Protagoras apparently recognized the importance of students understanding both sides of an issue in preparing to be active citizens.

The origins of academic debate contests date back to Ancient Greece.

The first intercollegiate debate in the English-speaking world took place in the early 1400s at Cambridge University among students from Cambridge and Oxford. The debating programs in Britain have always used a parliamentary format and have long been a training ground for future members of Parliament.

Immigrants to America in the 18th century brought their interest in speech and debate to the New World. Citizens created literary societies to discuss and debate important ideas. As a result, debate flourished in the colonial colleges. University students engaged in **disputations**, highly structured discussions of logical questions that became popular during the 19th century. "From the Spy Club at Harvard in 1722 to the Young Ladies Association, the first women's debate society, at Oberlin College in 1835, the one common thread in literary societies was student interest in debating important issues."[3]

Eventually, college debate societies began publicly to debate each other in formal contests during the late 1800s. These contests were very popular and attracted large audiences.[4] The debates often took an entire day, accompanied by considerable ritual and fanfare similar to contemporary sporting events. This interest in competitive debate increased steadily during the 20th century. The period from 1920 to 1946 was characterized by **contract debating**. A college debating team would send out contracts to other teams specifying details such as which team would argue what side of the proposition, the length and number of speeches, and how to select judges. Schools that participated in these contract debates would usually compete in one debate per day. Because contract debating was very time consuming due to all the negotiating that took place, it led to the creation of leagues and honor societies whose functions included standardizing rules and procedures. Although it would still take many years for all contest rules to be nationally standardized, debate honor societies such as Pi Kappa Delta and Delta Sigma Rho-Tau Kappa Alpha formed during the early 1900s still exist today.

ACADEMIC TOURNAMENT DEBATE

One of the most influential practices in intercollegiate debating was the introduction of the debate tournament format where a host school invited several colleges to send participants and judges. In 1923, Southwestern College in Winfield, Kansas, hosted the first debate tournament. However, the tournament format did not become universally popular until the late 1940s. In 1947, the U.S. Military Academy at West Point began the **National Debate Tournament** (NDT) and continued to host the tournament for 19 years. In 1967, the **American Forensic Association** (AFA) assumed responsibility for the NDT, which has been hosted by a different college each year since then.

Tournament debating brought a renewed emphasis on competitive debate and with it, several changes in terms of methods and techniques that governed the activity. In order to hold several rounds of debate in one or two days, the lengths of speeches were limited to 10 minutes for constructive speeches and 5 minutes for the rebuttals. Early tournaments used the three-speaker team, but later tournaments were responsible for the invention of the two-speaker system. Additionally, a national topic was selected for use during an entire academic year. There was also a loss of the popular audience. The real audience became the critic-judge.[5]

Debate continued to grow rapidly until the early 1970s. Unfavorable economic conditions during the 1970s significantly reduced the number of college debate programs. In recent years, continued economic downturns have again severely pinched higher education budgets. The resulting resource scarcity has led to the cutback or cancellation of many debate programs, especially at state-supported institutions.

In 2007, there were approximately 500 universities and colleges nationwide that participated in interscholastic debate. On any given weekend during the academic year, hundreds of college students across the nation are participating in some form of organized debate competition. Although this number represents fewer schools than 50 years ago, the number of participating schools has stabilized in recent years. College students active in debate can select from several popular debate formats that are currently available to them as part of their intercollegiate debate experience.

POPULAR DEBATE FORMATS

On any given weekend during the academic year, thousands of college students across the nation participate in some form of organized debate competition.

Although fewer universities and colleges participate in competitive debate compared to the 1960s, there are currently four popular intercollegiate formats offering competitive contests for students interested in debating. They include NDT debate, Cross-Examination Debate Association debate (CEDA), Lincoln–Douglas (LD) debate, and Parliamentary debate. Public debates held on college campuses represent a fifth format. Although public debates are highly valued, these events are not regulated by any of the national intercollegiate debate organizations and are usually not a key part of competitive interscholastic debate programs. We will briefly explain these five formats in the next few pages.

National Debate Tournament

Although the initials **NDT** stand for the national debate tournament (the oldest championship tournament for college debate), these initials are also synonymous with the competitive style of collegiate policy debate represented at tournaments held throughout the academic year. These tournaments take place almost every weekend from the end of September to mid-April by colleges and universities throughout the nation. Most tournaments offer six or eight preliminary rounds of competition in which a two-member team will debate an even number of rounds on both sides of the resolution. Depending on the size of the tournament, there will usually be three or four elimination rounds for the teams with the best preliminary record. Some debaters compete in as many as 20 tournaments a year.

NDT debate has traditionally argued policy propositions written by a national topic committee and voted on by college debate coaches. This topic is announced the summer before the academic debate season begins and is the only topic the debaters will argue during that school year. All the tournaments use an identical format; 10-minute constructive speeches, 5-minute rebuttal speeches and, beginning in 1974, 3-minute cross-examination periods were included after each constructive speech. One of the objectives of these weekly collegiate tournaments is to prepare a debate team to qualify for the NDT championship. Since only 64 teams can compete at the NDT championship, a team has to earn a "bid" through a district qualifying competition. A district is usually comprised of several states within a specific region, and only a limited number of slots are allocated to each district. Additional participants can also qualify through at-large invitations based on their successful debating records throughout the season. The NDT has always been considered the world series of academic debate where only the elite are able to qualify to compete in the national championship. Austin Freely compares the NDT to the "big dance" in collegiate basketball when he writes, "As in the National Collegiate Athletic Association (NCAA) basketball tournament, only a select number of teams are chosen to participate in the NDT."[6]

The NDT style of debate has frequently been criticized for the rapid speed in which debaters talk and the amount of research that must be done for teams to be able to compete successfully. As a result, today far fewer schools participate in the NDT format than they did years ago. In recent years, other educational debate formats have become more popular with colleges and universities.

Cross-Examination Debate Association

In 1971, the CEDA was created to provide an alternative to NDT debating—in part to meet a perceived need by placing greater emphasis on communication. Until 1974, CEDA exclusively employed cross-examination as a significant component of its debating format. Additionally, CEDA established two topics a year—one for first semester and a different one for second semester—as opposed to the single year topic of the NDT. Initially, CEDA selected non-NDT policy propositions, but by 1975 was using value propositions exclusively. In 1986, CEDA established a national championship tournament open to any CEDA member and by the late 1980s had surpassed the NDT as the most widely used mode of intercollegiate debating.[7]

However, in 1996, the fall CEDA topic was reselected for the spring topic, creating a single, yearlong proposition like NDT. By the mid-1990s, most CEDA debates involved discussions of policies and were very similar in content to those occurring among schools debating the NDT topic.[8] CEDA debaters had also adopted many of the same stylistic patterns as NDT debaters (rapid delivery, large quantities of evidence); the two debate groups were far more similar than distinct. In 1996, the NDT leadership communicated to CEDA that if the organization would select a yearlong policy proposition, NDT would adopt that proposition as well, creating a shared topic. CEDA agreed and essentially the "merger" of CEDA and NDT took place. Although the two groups still maintain separate ranking systems, schools can compete in both NDT and CEDA tournaments previously unavailable to them. Some teams compete in both the NDT, where they must qualify through a selection process, and the CEDA National Championship open to any team representing a member school.

Today, NDT and CEDA debate formats are very similar. Thus, the same criticisms of the NDT debating style are now apparent with the CEDA format as well. Because of this de facto merger in 1996, many university and college debate programs no longer participate in either of these formats. Instead, debate programs have turned to either LD or Parliamentary debate formats. Parliamentary debate, in particular, has experienced unprecedented growth in the past decade.

Lincoln–Douglas Debate

LD debate originated from the famous debates between Stephen A. Douglas and Abraham Lincoln in their race for the U.S. Senate during 1858. In these debates, which would frequently last more than 3 hours, the first speech lasted 1 hour, the next an hour and a half, and the final rebuttal a half hour. Stephen Douglas had no way of realizing that when he agreed to that series of joint appearances with Lincoln almost 150 years ago, he set in motion an increasingly popular debate format that would become an interscholastic competitive event at both the college and high school levels.

Whereas NDT and CEDA debate formats involve two-person teams opposing other two-person teams, LD is one debater against another. Teamwork and cooperation are very much a part of policy debate, while individual initiative and self-reliance are very much a part of LD debate. LD debate is a great alternative for the debater who cannot find a partner or simply prefers working solo. The LD debater can take greater personal pleasure in success, but has fewer people to blame for failure.[9] LD debate in high school utilizes only value propositions; however, policy propositions are used at the college level.

The LD debate format emerged as an alternative to the NDT and CEDA formats due to widespread dissatisfaction with rapid delivery, evidence presentation, and game playing.[10] Currently, the National Forensic Association at the collegiate level regulates LD debate. This organization views LD Debate as a one-person, persuasive, policy debate on traditional stock issues. It is primarily a communication event; rapid-fire delivery is antithetical to the purpose and intent of this event. Just like NDT and CEDA debate, LD has traditionally argued policy propositions written by a national topic committee and voted on by the college debate coaches. The topic is announced late summer before the academic debate season begins and is the only topic the LD debaters will argue during that school year. Time limits for LD debate are

- 1st affirmative. Constructive -   6 minutes
- cross-examination -   3 minutes
- 1st negative. Constructive -   7 minutes
- cross-examination -   3 minutes
- 1st affirmative. Rebuttal -   4 minutes
- 1st negative. Rebuttal -   6 minutes
- 2nd affirmative. Rebuttal -   3 minutes

A typical LD debate will last 32 minutes while an NDT or CEDA round of debate will last well over an hour. Three fewer speeches are given in LD debate. This event has experienced significant growth based on the number of new schools electing to participate in LD. Given the "renewed" commitment to LD as a communication activity, it is one of the few collegiate debate formats that genuinely reflect its historical legacy.

Parliamentary Debate

Academic parliamentary debate is closely modeled after the Oxford Union Debate practiced in British colleges, and is less structured than the formats discussed above. This form of debate may use fact, value, or policy propositions and allows for greater audience involvement. Teams comprised of two individuals receive their topics 15 minutes before the debate round begins, and there is a new topic for each round of debate during the tournament competition. Because debaters have a new proposition each round, the emphasis is on logic, reasoning, knowledge, and presentation skills, with less emphasis on the use of evidence and complex arguments. Propositions are stated from the perspective of the House: *"This House believes"* or *"This House would."* Topics are generally of two types: straight or abstract.[11] Straight resolutions define a specific topic for debate: "The United States should expand its development and/or use of nuclear power"; "The U.S. Federal Government should de-link the Federal Emergency Management Agency (FEMA) from the Department of Homeland Security." Abstract resolutions are broad topics that allow the government team to link the resolution to an infinite number of issues. Examples of abstract resolutions include, "This House Should Value Idealism Over Pragmatism, "This House Would Circle the Wagons" or "This House believes Existentially."

Academic parliamentary debate is modeled after the Oxford Union Debate practiced in many British colleges.

Once the preparation time is over and the debate begins, the speaking times are

- Prime Minister constructive   7 minutes
- Leader of Opposition constructive   8 minutes
- Member of Government constructive   8 minutes
- Member of Opposition constructive   8 minutes
- Leader of Opposition rebuttal   4 minutes
- Prime Minister rebuttal   5 minutes

There is no designated cross-examination period. Instead, **points of information** and **points of order** are available to the speakers. After the first minute and before the last minute of all constructive speeches, the opposing team may offer points of information to the speaker who holds the floor. The purpose of these statements or questions is to clarify a point the speaker is making, advance a point for the opposing team, or highlight a weakness in the other team's case. Points of information create a more interactive style of debate since they allow the opposing team to interrupt the speaker at an appropriate and often strategic time. Likewise, the speaker can refuse to take the point of information and, thus, maintain control of the allotted speaking time.

The speakers direct points of order to the judge. They are most frequently utilized during the rebuttal period to object to a new argument, or if the opposing team is misconstruing an argument. The judge must make an immediate ruling on the point of order and does not need to justify the decision he or she makes. The debaters are not allowed to discuss or object to the judge's ruling on a point of order. This procedure allows both teams the opportunity to highlight unfair strategies used by the opposing teams during rebuttal speeches.

Parliamentary debate format prohibits reading or citing evidence cards during a debate and instead focuses on various forms of support such as examples, common knowledge, analogies, and statistics that are referred to, but not read. A well-read individual will have no difficulty finding examples to support arguments without having to read evidence cards in the round. Additionally, with a new topic for each debate, a parliamentary debater will research a wide range of topics rather than one specific topic.

This style of debate has experienced unprecedented growth in the past decade compared to the other three educational formats. Parliamentary debate started in the early 1990s with 52 teams represented at the first national championship tournament in 1994. In 2007, more than 200 teams competed at the national tournament and several teams had to be turned away due to space limitations.

Public Debate

Many universities and colleges have debating clubs or societies that sponsor public debates conducted in front of a general audience of students and community members. These debates could be against a rival institution, students versus faculty, or candidates running for student government positions. The public debate format can supplement an interscholastic competitive program or may be the only debate program an institution can afford. Debate conducted before audience groups require that the debater undertake a careful audience analysis and make specific preparation in terms of the audience. Communicating arguments in a style in which audiences can understand and engage is vitally important to the success of the public debate format. The number of speeches and format followed will depend on the audience situation and will vary for each public debate.

It is important to remember that audience members may attend a debate for a variety of reasons. Some may want to understand the topic of the debate better and want to gain more information about a specific issue. Others may want the debate process to assist them in making a decision about the resolution. Finally, others may be curious about debate as a both a competitive and public speaking activity. The fundamental goal or objective of most public debate is to help educate audience members, regardless of the reasons they attend a public debate.

Long-time debate coach and argumentation scholar, Dr. Austin Freely summarized this philosophy when he stated:

Although it is hoped that debates presented before public audiences will be both interesting and profitable for the audience, they should never be regarded as purely entertainment. Debates presented before public audiences should be treated as an opportunity to educate students about audience analysis and to educate the audience about debate.[12]

Judging Tournament Debates

As judges of such televised talent shows as *American Idol* and *Dancing with the Stars,* audiences are always concerned with who won or who received the lowest vote total in last night's competition. Tremendous fanfare precedes the climatic announcement of the final winner of the competition. Although there is never the same level of excitement and fanfare for who won a specific classroom or tournament debate compared to reality television shows, the final decision or outcome is still exceedingly important to the individuals involved in the debate. Therefore, the role played by the debate judge is integral to a thorough understanding and appreciation of the debate as an educational activity. Such questions as "What is the role of a debate judge? Who judge debates?" and "How do judges decide who wins or loses a debate?" will now be addressed.

What is the Role of the Judge?

Debate involves two separate goals: competition and education. The judge or critic is intimately involved with both aspects. Neither one can be allowed to overshadow the other since each is equally important. In order to foster competition, it is necessary for the judge to maintain the fairness of each round. The most obvious aspect of fairness is impartiality. A fair and impartial judge creates a level playing field upon which the debate occurs. The assigned judge must ignore the reputation of the school, the individual debater, or coach. Most importantly, a judge must evaluate the debate on its own merits, voting only on the arguments the debaters made—not on the arguments the judge wished the debaters had made or arguments the judge made in his or her mind. Judges should never require the students to debate them rather than the opposing team.

As important as fairness is to competition, judges have an equal commitment to the education of the debaters. All judges become teachers the moment they enter a debate round with the objective of identifying which team will win or lose. Beyond rendering a decision, it is critical that judges complete a ballot that provides specific information that the debaters can use to improve. This includes not only identifying areas that need improvement, but detailed suggestions for how the debaters can accomplish those necessary improvements. The judge's primary goal as an educator is to provide constructive recommendations in a way that motivates students to become better debaters.

In order for an individual to be both a fair adjudicator and effective educator, he or she has two basic responsibilities while listening to a debate: to flow the debate and to write a clear ballot. As discussed earlier in the text, note taking in debate is called *"flowing"* because one takes notes in such a way as to follow the flow of arguments as they are extended through the debate. The flow sheet for the debate round is essential if a judge is going to render a fair and impartial decision based on the information presented in the round. No judge, despite what he or she may claim, can remember each argument over the course of an entire debate. Having a complete record of the arguments advanced in a debate is also vital to the educational function of the activity.

The second responsibility is for a judge to make a decision and justify it. The decision, as part of the education process of debate, should be reported in a manner (as mentioned previously) that contributes to the students' education. This reporting may occur in the form of an oral critique or a carefully prepared written ballot. Ideally, a judge should provide both. The ballot a judge writes should explain clearly the reasons why one team was more successful than the other team. The contents of the ballot should include a list of the crucial arguments, stating which team carried each argument and why. Presenting the reasons helps determine whether the decision is fair, and the ballot acts as a means of justifying a decision to the debaters. This justification process is important because as one survey noted, more than 85% of all debaters think they won any given round of debate. Of course, only 50% can win. As a result, the ballot functions as a pedagogical tool providing feedback to debaters as to how to address specific issues, thereby ensuring that they will be more successful in future debates.

Who are the Judges?

Each school entering a debate tournament is obligated to provide officials to judge the debates. These judges may be members of the school's debate coaching staff, faculty, former debaters who are now alumni, and in some cases, community members. Judges generally fall into three types: Lay judges, former debaters/former coaches, coach judges.

Lay judges are any judges who do not have any background or very limited background in debate. Lay judges may be in professions related to debate—for example, attorneys or courtroom judges—or they may have little experience in debate such as community leaders or parents of debaters. Lay judges are much more likely to judge Parliamentary, Lincoln–Douglas, or public debates. Rarely do lay judges render decisions in either NDT or CEDA debate rounds.

A large number of tournament judges may be ex-debaters who have graduated from college. Debate tournaments require a large number of judges, and such individuals serve as valuable resources when adjudicators must be hired. Former debate coaches, many who are faculty in college departments, may also be invited to judge if their university is hosting a tournament.

Coach judges or graduate students who are assisting with debate programs comprise a major portion of the tournament judging pool. Each school must usually provide one judge for every two teams or LD debaters they enter in a tournament. Therefore, most coaches are expected to judge in order to meet their school's judging obligation.

Successful debaters become very adept at adapting to a variety of judging styles. For example, lay judges require debaters to speak very slowly, clearly, and avoid using debate jargon. On the other end of the spectrum, coach judges have listened to countless debates per week on the topic and may have heard literally thousands of debates during their career. They are extremely familiar with the debate topic and current argumentation theory. Therefore, debaters will want to be thorough, efficient, and particularly logical in front of such judges.

How Do Judges Make Decisions?

Ultimately, judges of academic debates must answer the question, "Which team did the better debating? In order to answer this question, judges apply their knowledge of argumentation and debate in order to evaluate each substantive issue emerging from the debate. However, the weight given to each argument may vary depending on an individual's judging philosophy or **judging paradigm**. Judging paradigms refer to the model the judge uses to evaluate the debate round. This model illustrates how judges view debates by identifying which types of issues will be prioritized in terms of the way a judge will cast a decision at the end of a debate. The three of the most common paradigms used by debate judges will be discussed: debating skills judge, stock issues judge, and policy maker judge.

A **skills judge** focuses on the skills listed on a debate ballot: analysis, reasoning, evidence, organization, refutation, delivery, and cross-examination, and carefully evaluates which team has performed better with regard to each of these skills. Skills judges use their knowledge about argumentation and debate to determine which skills were instrumental in persuading them to vote for a certain side. For example, one team's communication skills or its refutation skills in explaining a critical issue is so superior to its opponents that it becomes decisive in terms of a final decision.

The **stock issues judge** emphasizes stock issues of harm, inherency, workability, and cost. In order to win, the affirmative side has to win all the stock issues, but the negative needs to win only one stock issue. The affirmative is not required to win every argument in the debate, but must win each stock issue.

The **policymaker judge** evaluates the affirmative's policy system (the proposed plan) compared to the negative's policy system (a defense of the status quo, a minor repair, a counter plan) and then makes a decision as to whether or not the affirmative offers a better policy option. This type of judge would also have to determine if the affirmative plan is viable (that it can indeed work). A policy maker judge essentially employs a cost-benefit analysis comparing the advantages or benefits a new policy offers over the present system compared to the possible disadvantages or "costs" to adopting the new proposal.

Although these represent three of the most common philosophical approaches to judging debates, they certainly do not represent all the decision rules judges will employ when evaluating arguments in a debate round. In fact, there may be as many ways to judge a debate, as there are judges.[13] In order to facilitate the ability for debaters to adapt to the preferences of specific judges, they should ask a judge before beginning a debate to explain his or her judging paradigm. Many tournaments, including NDT and CEDA nationals, compile booklets publishing each judge's philosophy statement. Teams receive this booklet as part of their registration materials, and most will carefully read the judging philosophy before debating in front of that individual.

Judges are human and many different factors can determine the outcome of each individual debate. There are times that judges will deviate from their judging philosophy—either intentionally or unintentionally. However, research shows that the majority of judges in the academic debate community view debates with extraordinary consensus, regardless of their stated judging philosophies.[14] A group of debate scholars at the first National Development Conference on Debate outlined what they believed was the ideal "model" for evaluating a debate when they wrote that "The judge should value content above delivery and substance above technique. The stronger position on the issue should prevail and the more credible evidence should prevail over a greater quantity of evidence having less probative value."[15]

Not all contemporary debate judges adhere to this decision-rule. However, all debate and argumentation scholars would agree that debate has been and continues to be an integral component of a strong liberal education. The debate judge will always serve as a crucial mechanism for fulfilling the educational mission of this activity as envisioned by the ancient Greek, "Protagoras" . . . the Father of Debate

SUMMARY

Debate has stood the test of time as a valuable educational tool. It has changed considerably since its emergence in ancient Greece, continuing through the 19th century to the contemporary debate practices of the 21st century. Different formats, events, and theories have all combined to make competitive debate far different from the public contests of the 1880s. Currently, several interscholastic debate formats are available to students who, after engaging in classroom debates, may wish to get more involved in competitive debate. These popular formats include NDT policy debate, CEDA debate, LD debate, Parliamentary debate, and Public Audience debates sponsored by student groups located on campus. Each format has its own distinct rules, philosophy, and focus depending on the needs of students. NDT and CEDA policy debates are team activities requiring a substantive commitment from students since they require extensive months of research on a single topic. Parliamentary debate, also a team event, provides a competitive opportunity to students who are interested in arguing from a common base of knowledge on a variety of current events or philosophical topics that span multiple disciplines, with a focus on both effective communication and argumentation skills. LD debate is an individual competition rather than a team event using a policy proposition with the primary focus on developing communication skills. Finally, public debates sponsored through various student campus organizations offer students an opportunity to debate in front of audiences, thereby gaining valuable experience in public communication.

An important component of any academic debate format is the judge or critic who determines the outcome of the debate. Judges can be community members with no formal debate training, former debaters who have graduated, argumentation scholars, or well-versed debate coaches. Each judge tries to render a fair and impartial decision at the conclusion of the debate, based on his or her individual judging philosophy.

NOTES

1   Freeley, A., & Steinberg, D. (2000). *Argumentation and debate: Critical thinking for reasoned decision making* (10th ed., p. 15). Belmont, CA: Wadsworth.

2   Thonseen, L., & Baird, A. (1948). *Speech criticism.* New York, NY: Ronald Press.

3 Delancey, C., & Halford, R. (1990). Intercollegiate audience debating: Quo Vadis. *Argumentation and Advocacy, 27,* 49.

4 Nichols, E. (1936). A historical sketch of intercollegiate debating. *Quarterly Journal of Speech, XXII,* 213

5 Faules, D., & Rieke, R. (1968). *Directing forensics: Debate and contest speaking* (p. 15). Scranton, PA: International Textbook.

6 Freeley, & Steinberg, p. 20.

7 Ibid.

8 Ibid.

9 Phillips, L., Hicks, W., & Springer, D. (2000). *Basic debate* (p. 156). Chicago, IL: National Textbook.

10 Bartanen, M. (1994). *Teaching & directing forensics* (p. 107). Scottsdale, AZ: Gorsuch Scarisbrick.

11 Knapp, T., & Galizio, L. (1990). *Parliamentary debate: A guide to public argument* (p. 3). New York, NY: Addison Wesley.

12 Freeley, & Steinberg, p. 324.

13 Ibid., p. 305.

14 Cross, J., & Matlon, R. (1978). An analysis of judging philosophies in academic debate. *Journal of the American Forensics Association, 15,* 110–123.

15 McBath, J. (Ed.). (1975). *Forensics as communication* (p. 30). Skokie, IL: National Textbook.

Chapter 9

Argumentation and Debate in Different Professional Contexts

CHAPTER OUTLINE

KEY TERMS

Attack Ad
Beyond a Reasonable Doubt
Common Law
Constitutional Law
Credibility
Discovery Period

Expert Testimony
Fields of Argument
Negative Campaign
Physical Evidence
Preponderance of the Evidence
Statutory Law

We began this textbook by making the claim that argumentation and debate play a vital role in our society today. The central role of argument can be seen in professional contexts, or **fields of argument**, where policy making institutions use argumentation and debate to create policies that directly impact how we live, how we consume material goods, and how we are governed. The argumentation that takes place in professional contexts often includes a judge, audience, or group with the power to make a decision based on the arguments they hear. In a legal context, attorneys make arguments for or against convicting a person of a crime. In a business context, corporations make arguments to convince investors and the public that they are a profitable company offering a desirable service or product. In political campaigns, candidates make arguments to convince the public that they are the best choice to represent the public's interests as a governing official.

This concluding chapter will provide an overview of the way people use argumentation to reach their goals in different professional contexts. More specifically, we explain how the principles and concepts of argumentation discussed in preceding chapters are implemented and employed in three professional contexts: law, business, and politics.

ARGUMENTATION AND LAW

As we discussed in Chapter 1, the roots of argumentation are as ancient as the beginning of civilization as scholars and philosophers from different cultures practiced, developed, and studied how people use rhetoric to influence others in their developing societies.[1] One of the earliest professional contexts in which people practiced argumentation was the legal field, specifically in a court of law. Ancient civilizations like Greece, where a new type of governance called democracy was developing, established courts where individuals represented themselves.

Argumentation in the legal field dates back to ancient times.

Today, the rules and procedures governing the American legal system are complex as they vary between federal and state, from state to state, and between localities.[2] In addition, the argumentation used in the legal system differs from one type of case to another. For example, in criminal cases, the prosecutor's argument must meet the *burden of proof* standard that the defendant is guilty **beyond a reasonable doubt**, meaning that the argument is so convincing you would rely and act upon it without hesitation in the most important of your own affairs (see Chapter 5). In civil cases, the burden is lower as the argument only has to demonstrate a preponderance of evidence. A **preponderance of evidence** means the argument presents enough evidence that the fact or facts is more likely than not.

Since the legal system is composed of a multitude of rules, procedures, and cases, we will focus on some general principles that transcend the various legal contexts.

Decision Makers in Law

Regardless of the type of case, there are two primary decision makers in law: judges and jurors. Judges play the important role of interpreting and applying constitutional, statutory, and common law in courts. **Constitutional** and **Statutory laws** are created and written by the legislative branch of the federal, state, or local government. Meanwhile, **common law** originates from past judicial decisions. These legal parameters guide judges in rendering decisions and/or instructing the jury how to apply the law to their decisions; the system also guides judges in determining if a case has been properly brought before the court, if a *prima facie* case has been established, and if evidence has been properly admitted.

Jurors represent the second type of decision maker in law. Jurors have the important task of evaluating evidence, determining what evidence to accept as fact, and making a decision on whether an argument meets the burden of proof.

Forms of Argumentation in Law

Deductive arguments dominate legal argumentation. As we discussed in Chapter 2, in a *deductive argument* we reason from a general principle to a specific conclusion. In addition, the claim must follow from the premises; therefore, the claim in a deductive argument is either *valid* (we must accept it) or *invalid*. To illustrate, consider the following:

Major premise: *Embezzlement is a crime.*

Minor premise: *Jack embezzled money.*

Claim: *Jack committed a crime.*

In this *categorical syllogism*, we must accept the claim if we accept the premises. As illustrated above, legal argumentation attempts to establish claims that demonstrate either guilt or innocence based on an undisputed major premise.

Forms of Evidence in Law

In any court case, deductive arguments need support material in order to verify the claims that are made. Skillful lawyers attempt to use the most compelling evidence in which to meet their burden. For brevity, we comment on three types of support that are used commonly in law: facts, physical evidence, and expert testimony.

In both criminal and civil cases, lawyers attempt to identify important *facts* that prove the claims in their arguments. Frequently, the identification of facts enables lawyers to establish the motive for the crime. For example, if a lawyer were attempting to show that the defendant embezzled money, the lawyer would need to establish motive (why he did it). If the lawyer presents evidence that the defendant had a gambling problem, this fact could establish motive for the crime: the gambling problem may explain why the defendant stole money.

The physical evidence in the case sometimes bolsters claims. In the hypothetical embezzlement case mentioned above, the physical evidence could include the defendant's laptop, e-mails, financial transactions, and bank statements that the lawyer would introduce in a trial. Physical evidence, especially when there are no eyewitnesses, is a powerful form of support to prove claims in a court of law.

Another important type of evidence used in law is **expert testimony**. An individual is considered an expert if he or she is widely recognized as a credible source of knowledge and whose opinion is acknowledged as having authority in his or her field. In a trial, lawyers attempt to identify experts who can speak as an authority on an issue. For example, it is common in murder cases for a defense lawyer to call an expert psychologist to the stand to testify on matters pertaining to the mental state of the defendant at the time of the murder. If expert testimony can convince the jurors that the defendant was insane at the time of the killing, it could mean the difference between a first-degree murder conviction and that of a lesser charge.

Ethics and Law

The argumentation and forms of support executed in a court of law adhere to specific rules and regulations in order to ensure a fair trial. For example, there are specific rules that determine the admissibility of evidence in a case. Law enforcement must properly secure and handle evidence from the crime scene. Any evidence that was not gathered legally (such as interviewing a suspect without his or her lawyer present or failing to document and label a piece of evidence) is not admissible in court. Once a lawyer collects the evidence, there is a **discovery period** where both sides can request to review the evidence and documents related to the case. At this time, both sides must identify the witnesses they plan to call in the case.

In addition to the rules governing the admissibility of evidence, is the code of conduct that defines the professional responsibilities of judges and lawyers. Judges are not to hear cases in which they have a conflict of interest. Examples of conflicts of interest for judges include hearing a case in which they have a financial interest, hearing a case in which they were involved as a lawyer, or hearing a case in which they are related to (or friends with) persons who are involved in the litigation.

Lawyers also have a code of conduct. Some of the ethical standards that lawyers must follow include the following stipulations: not obstructing another party's access to evidence, not altering or concealing documents, not assisting a witness to testify falsely, not revealing information relating to the representation of an individual, and not abusing legal procedure. Adherence to these ethical standards ensures fairness and due process in a court of law.

ARGUMENTATION AND BUSINESS

As in the law, argumentation in business is dynamic and complex. In addition, business is a very competitive enterprise since corporations will go to great lengths to create advertisements to influence individuals to buy a specific product or service. The competitive nature of business is demonstrated by the fact that we as consumers are exposed to over 5,000 persuasive messages a day to influence us to buy a product or service[3]

Argumentation in business persuades individuals to consume products, services, and ideas.

The competitive nature of business underscores the importance of ethics in the corporate world. Ethics are important in business because there is a fine line between what an acceptable persuasive message is and what it is not. For example, a few years ago, Domino's Pizza was an upstart regional company that introduced a guarantee of delivering a pizza in 30 minutes or the pizza would be free. The popular slogan "30 minutes or the pizza is free" is credited with Domino's growth into a national chain. However, the practice was not without ethical risks—specifically drivers getting into accidents in their effort to beat the 30-minute guarantee. After a fatal accident, the then CEO of the company decided to end the practice. Ethically, the desire to fulfill a guarantee was not worth the risks of losing a person's life.

Decision Makers in Business

The Domino's example illustrates the importance of ethics in business. In fact, accounting firms and security analysts help ensure that businesses operate ethically. Both underscore two presumptions in business: accounting firms are independent entities that verify the accuracy and reliability of data provided by the business, and analysts provide reliable information on the success of the business. Analysts also project how well the business will perform in the future.

Forms of Argumentation in Business

In Chapter 2, we identified some of the major types of reasoning used in arguments. Not surprisingly, corporations use a multitude of arguments to persuade consumers to buy their product or service. Although the types of arguments are endless, we focus on some of the most frequently used types of arguments in business.

One primary way that businesses make arguments is comparing and contrasting past and present performance. Companies make arguments that their present performance is better than past performance during some range of time, whether quarterly or annually. When corporate profits meet or exceed expectations, it bolsters the claims of the successful status of the company.

Reasoning by cause bases the truth of a claim on a cause–effect relationship between two things, one leading to the other. Whenever there is a factor that affects sales, there is a need to determine its cause. A number of factors such as labor problems, higher transportation causes, and weather conditions can cause a decrease in profit.

Reasoning by cause is illustrated by the Big Three automakers Ford, GM, and DaimlerChrysler. Each automaker during the past decade has struggled to adjust to the changing auto market. Among the major causes for the decline in sales include foreign automakers, higher fuel prices, health care costs, retirement pensions, and labor costs. These causes have spurred each automaker to create new vehicles such as hybrid automobiles that get better gas mileage in order to compete with foreign auto manufacturers.

Reasoning by sign bases the truth of a claim on a relationship between two things where one indicates the other. Although we generally hesitate to assume a causal relationship between a sign and what the sign indicates, this type of reasoning closely resembles effect-to-cause reasoning. For example, the financial numbers found on the New York Stock Exchange represents one indicator of the state of the economy and future performance of companies. People read the value of a company's stock as a sign of investor confidence in the future performance of the company.

Forms of Evidence in Business

Some of the arguments we discussed represent vital ways businesses convey to the public and investors the vibrancy of its corporation. It is a vibrancy that is dependent upon the business earning profits; therefore, corporations strategically plan how to create persuasive messages that will influence consumers to buy their product or service. In Chapter 4, we discussed the various ways support is used in argumentation. Here we identify a few common forms of support used in the field of business argumentation.

Examples are specific cases that illustrate a claim. Corporations use examples constantly to highlight how a product or service is necessary for a consumer. For example, when Ford created hybrid versions of the Escape, Ford demonstrated that it could create fuel-efficient SUVs like its competitors.

Statistics are numbers used to represent information. The corporate world is saturated with the use of numbers, figures, and charts to show the health of the business along with explaining how a particular company (or its product) is better than its competition. For example, the car insurance company, GEICO, is known for its offbeat caveman commercials. Part of the underlying argument is if we are smarter than cavemen why haven't we switched our car insurance to a cheaper but just as effective company? Along with its slogan, "Even a caveman can do it," its commercials always end with the phrase, "GEICO, fifteen minutes can save you fifteen percent or more on your car insurance." The statistic is used to motivate the audience members to call GEICO to get a better rate on their car insurance and, hopefully, switch to GEICO.

When speakers use *testimony* as a form of support, it is dependent on the credibility of the person giving his or her opinion about a product or service (see below). Testimony creates a personal connection with the audience by conveying the spokesperson's actual experiences with the product or service.

As we mentioned in the previous paragraph, credibility is closely related to testimony. **Credibility** is the quality of being believable and trustworthy, based upon the credentials, education, experience, integrity, and reputation of the individual. Credibility underscores *reasoning by authority* where the truth of a claim depends on the credibility of an external source. A business might argue, for example, that a specific product is environmentally safe and has been endorsed by the Sierra Club. The reasoning asserts that the source, the Sierra Club, an environmental monitoring organization, is both competent and trustworthy.

Ethics and Business

The competitiveness of business results in tactics of argumentation that attempt to influence individuals to consume specific products or services. Business argumentation, while effective, sometimes pushes ethical standards to the limit. Not surprisingly, ethical misconduct can arise in many contexts such as business philosophy, social responsibility, environmental protection, corporate-to-corporate relations, political contributions, and marketing.

In business, the word of advice for consumers is "let the buyer beware." Business argumentation commonly uses questionable strategies such as omitting important information, downplaying negative information, diverting, and confusing in order to influence the consumer. For this reason, business practitioners sometimes equate ethics in business with legality—if the claim is not against the law then the argumentation is ethical. Often, it is not until we catch a company such as Enron, which used accounting omissions that over inflated the company's stock (and thus led to the company's collapse), that we discover how unethical their argumentation was.

ARGUMENTATION AND POLITICS

Politics is a third area where argumentation is prominent. Argumentation and debate fuels the political process, from running a campaign to creating legislation. Furthermore, the media age of 24-hour news coverage, Internet bloggers, political interest groups, and political operatives has made argumentation a perpetual political debate.

Extensive media coverage has also heightened the use of showmanship and sound bites in an effort to control and persuade the public toward a specific agenda. For example, in the spring of 2007, congress debated whether to continue the war in Iraq by passing President Bush's funding measure. House Minority Leader John Boehner (R-OH) wept during his speech to persuade members of congress to pass the funding measure. Boehner's weeping was repeated throughout the media, which appealed to the public's emotions to support the troops and thus the spending request made by the president.

Similar to law and business, the political realm contains many contexts and procedures for political argumentation. We will focus on one type of political argumentation—political campaigns.

Decision Makers in Politics

The media age has not only affected the argumentation that is used in politics but it has redefined the important decision makers in politics. Traditionally, the political parties (namely, political bosses or chairpersons) had the power to handpick candidates and provide the necessary financial and organizational support to help the candidate win the party's nomination. However, changes in political campaigns and primaries have shifted the power from the political bosses to political consultants. In fact, political consultants have more influence in shaping a candidate's message, strategy, and governance than the candidate's party.[4] Political consultants are politically savvy individuals who are able to gauge public opinion, political issues, and the candidate's persona to create a message and strategy that will resonate with the public and thus help the candidate win election.

Campaign managers of the candidate function in addition to the political consultants. While political consultants focus upon strategy and message, the campaign manager coordinates the candidate's staff. In other words, campaign managers oversee the political structure that a candidate needs to win an election; they coordinate the candidate's communication department (such as public relations and advertising), fundraising, technology department (candidate's website), and field department (local organizers, volunteer coordinators, and get-out-the-vote volunteers).

The ultimate decision maker, however, in the political campaign is the voter. After all the campaigning, advertising, debates, and voter turnout efforts, the public exercises its right to vote for the candidate of its choice. Oftentimes exit-poll data is collected to determine if any trends have emerged from the election that can help political consultants, campaign managers, and candidates in the next election.

Forms of Argumentation in Political Campaigns

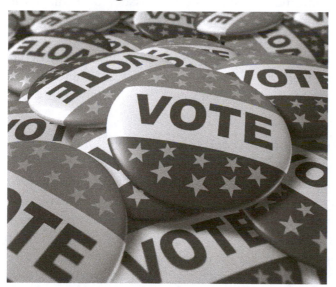

Political campaigns are known for the use of argumentation for or against a candidate.

Political campaigns are dynamic events that include the creation of a sustained message through various channels such as speeches, debates, television and radio ads, mailings, Internet, phone calls, campaign staff, and voter turnout efforts. Candidates have to be able to raise money in order to get their message out to the public. If a candidate is able to raise more money than was projected, it serves as a sign that the candidate has gained "traction" and his or her message is gaining appeal with the public. Whether the campaign is a national, state or local race, fundraising is a huge endeavor. In addition to the money that must be raised for a campaign, the candidate must create an effective message that resonates and ultimately influences the public to vote for his or her candidacy. We discuss three recurring forms of argumentation that are part of any campaign: issues and images, the people, and storytelling.

Campaigns consist of issues and images. The issues and images of candidates in a campaign are interrelated. It is difficult to separate issues and images because people tend to "personalize" the campaign by analyzing the person's character in relation to the issues. Rhetorical scholar, Lloyd Bitzer argued that the image of the candidate is more influential than the issues in the campaign because candidates often create messages and ads in which they campaign on their character.[5]

Many recent cases exemplify the salience of the image in political campaigns. For example, when Ronald Reagan ran for president in 1980, many perceived him as a "wild" cowboy who could not be trusted as commander in chief. However, given the context of then President Carter's unpopularity (a poor economy, energy crisis, and hostages in Iran), Reagan projected confidence to the American public by articulating that it was "Morning in America." Reagan rode his message of patriotism and American pride to a landslide election in 1980.

Similarity, 12 years later, a young governor from Arkansas, Bill Clinton, through his charisma and domestic agenda connected with a public unlike Reagan's successor, then President George H.W. Bush. One of the enduring images from the 1992 presidential campaign was a disengaged Bush looking down at his watch during a presidential debate. In addition, Bush was not able to respond to an audience member's question of the cost of a gallon of milk. The two images inferred that Bush was aloof and not sympathetic to the average American. Clinton's message of "It's the economy, stupid" enabled him win election to the White House in 1992.

The 2000 presidential election also demonstrated the power of image. Although Al Gore and George W. Bush shared the same pedigree (both came from political families, both came from wealth, and both went to Ivy League schools), their images were constructed differently in the media. Gore was constructed as the intellectual who was stiff, distinct, and lacking personality, while Bush was depicted as the common guy who was a "compassionate conservative." The images of the two heavily overshadowed the issues of the campaign as George W. Bush was determined the winner of the contested 2000 election.

Campaigns engage the people. Underlying the interrelationship between issues and images is the strategy of the candidate to win the election. All candidates attempt to appeal to the electorate by articulating that they are the leaders who will best advance the policies that the people desire. Scholar Michael McGee argued that terms like "the people" and "the public" are myths constructed by candidates to make it seem as if they have the support of all the people. By articulating "the people," candidates imply that they understand what the people want and that they should represent the people.[6]

Campaigns involve storytelling. Along with being able to speak for the people, the candidate must be able to construct a message that is simple enough for people to accept and understand. Candidates have to articulate a message that contains important issues, images, and references to "the people" within a dynamic and powerful *narrative.* For Barack Obama, his story, reflected the changing demographics of America—from his multiethnic background to his diverse upbringing. Many could identify with his story of "hard work leads to success" as he was raised by his mother as a single parent (and later raised by his grandparents) to go on to law school (and become the President of the *Harvard Law Review).* His story included his work as a community organizer and Senator. These achievements appealed to many and helped propel Obama to the presidency.

Forms of Evidence in Political Campaigns

One of the most powerful types of evidence used by candidates is an *example.* Similar to business argumentation, candidates point to their past record and accomplishments in order to define their policies, illustrate their style of governance, and make the argument for future action. Candidates point to their experience through examples to explain why they should be elected.

Implied in the forms of argumentation (issues and images, the people, and storytelling), is the *credibility* of the candidate. In politics, the credibility of the candidate is crucial in order to be elected. Voters want to be able to trust and believe their elected officials. Once elected, the credibility of the candidate with the public can rise and fall within the political context. Several brief examples illustrate this point. After the first Gulf War, George H.W. Bush had some of the highest approval ratings of any president in the modern era. However, a few months later, during his reelection campaign, his approval ratings plummeted (due to the economy and his lackluster campaign and debates), as he lost to Clinton. Clinton's approval ratings dropped with the failed universal health-care bill and rose during the Lewinsky scandal. George W. Bush's approval ratings were high after 9/11 but fell during the prolonged occupation of Iraq.

Ethics and Political Campaigns

Modern campaigns are very competitive endeavors as candidates, their political staff, and their parties attempt to construct and sustain messages designed to win an election. The high stakes of a political campaign often results in questionable argumentation as part of a candidate's **negative campaign** to smear an opposing candidate. Campaign ethics represent a troublesome part of politics. Although candidates often pledge to run "clean" campaigns, in reality, **attack ads** tend to dominate modern campaigns. These "hit pieces" create a negative image of the opposing candidate by distorting his or her image and record, taking quotations out of context, making ad hominem attacks, and using guilt by association.

Sometimes the candidate creates these negative ads, other times independent groups create them on behalf of the candidate. One of the most prominent independent groups was the Swift Boat Veterans for Truth. The Swift Boat Veterans for Truth ran negative ads during John Kerry's presidential campaign in 2004. The controversial ads attacked Kerry's service and the military medals he won in Vietnam. Since these groups are not affiliated officially with the campaign, there is little the candidate can do to prevent their ads. More troublesome is the fact that any group with the money can create an ad (whether accurate or not) and influence an election or political appointment whether the group represents the will of the people or not.

SUMMARY

In this chapter, we have taken a brief overview of how argumentation applies to professional contexts: specifically the realms of law, business, and politics. Each of these professional contexts, while complex and multifaceted, has some core themes in which argumentation is used to make legal, business, and political arguments. Regardless of the specified nature of the argument, they are built upon the principles we have conveyed in this textbook—through meticulous research, the construction of argumentation based on solid evidence and reasoning, and effective public speaking skills. These are principles that produce compelling and effective arguments regardless of the context.

NOTES

1 See Lipson, C. S., & Brinkley, R. A. (Eds.). (2004). *Rhetoric before and beyond the Greeks*. Albany, NY: SUNY Press; Jackson, R. L., & Richardson, E. B. (Eds.). (2003). *Understanding African American rhetoric*. New York, NY: Routledge.

2 Newell, S. E., & Rieke, R. D. (1986). A practical reasoning approach to legal doctrine. *Journal of American Forensic Association, 22,* 212–222.

3 Larson, C. (2001). *Persuasion: Reception and responsibility* (9th ed.). Belmont, CA: Wadsworth.

4 Doherty, J. W. (2006). The hidden network: Political consultants form party infrastructure. *Campaigns & Elections, 27,* 39–42.

5 Bitzer, L. (1981). Political rhetoric. In D. Nimmo & K. Sanders (Eds.), *Handbook of political communication* (pp. 225–248). Beverly Hills, CA: SAGE.

6 McGee, M. (1975). In search of "the people": A rhetorical alternative. *The Quarterly Journal of Speech, 61,* 235–249.

Argumentation Activities

ARGUMENTATIVENESS SCALE

Name _____   Date _____

Indicate how often each statement is true for you by placing the appropriate number in the blank to the left of the statement. If the statement is ALMOST NEVER TRUE for you, place a **1** in the blank. If the statement is RARELY TRUE for you, place a **2** in the blank. If the statement is OCCA-SIONALLY TRUE for you, place a **3** in the blank. If the statement is OFTEN TRUE for you, place a **4** in the blank. If the statement is ALWAYS TRUE for you place a **5** in the blank.

_____   **1.** While in an argument, I worry that the person I am arguing with will form a negative opinion of me.

_____   **2.** Arguing over controversial issues improves my intelligence.

_____   **3.** I enjoy avoiding arguments.

_____   **4.** I am energetic and enthusiastic when I argue.

_____   **5.** Once I finish an argument, I promise myself that I will not get into another.

_____   **6.** Arguing with a person creates more problems for me than it solves.

_____   **7.** I have a pleasant, good feeling when I win a point in an argument.

_____   **8.** When I finish arguing with someone, I feel nervous and upset.

_____   **9.** I enjoy a good argument over a controversial issue.

_____   **10.** I get an unpleasant feeling when I realize I am about to get into an argument.

_____   **11.** I enjoy defending my point of view on an issue.

_____   **12.** I am happy when I keep an argument from happening.

_____   **13.** I do not like to miss the opportunity to argue a controversial issue.

_____   **14.** I prefer being with people who rarely disagree with me.

_____   **15.** I consider an argument as an exciting intellectual challenge.

_____   **16.** I find myself unable to think of effective points during an argument.

_____ **17.** I feel refreshed and satisfied after an argument on a controversial issue.

_____ **18.** 1 have the ability to do well in an argument.

_____ **19.** I try to avoid getting into argument.

_____ **20.** I feel excitement when I expect that a conversation I am in is leading to an argument.

Scoring the Argumentativeness Scale

1. Add your scores on items: 2,4,7,9,11,13,15,17,18,20.
2. Add 60 to the sum obtained in step 1.
3. Add your scores on items: 1,3,5,6,8,10,12,14,16,19.
4. To compute your argumentativeness score, subtract the total obtained in step 3 from the total obtained in step 2.

Interpretation

High in argumentativeness	73–100
Moderate in argumentativeness	56–72
Low in argumentativeness	20–55

Some Research Findings

A number of studies have been done which indicate that argumentativeness is a positive personality trait (as operationalized above). But this should not be confused with the undesirable trait known as verbal aggressiveness (the desire to attack another person verbally).

Persons who score high in argumentativeness:

1. Tend to show increased interest in learning.
2. Generally are less egocentric in their thinking.
3. Demonstrate more skill in problem solving.
4. Are rated as being more credible speakers.
5. Are respected more by their superiors.
6. Have greater communication competence.
7. Are more difficult to provoke into aggression

For more information about this topic, see Infante, D. A. (1988). *Arguing Constructively*. Prospect Heights, ILL: Waveland Press.

REASONING MATCHING QUIZ

___

Name _____   Date _____

Indicate the type of reasoning used in each argument below.

A. Authority
B. Definition
C. Cause
D. Sign

___

E. Analogy

F. Generalization

G. Not an argument

1. _____ Republican Presidents can't be trusted. Richard Nixon lied to the American people about the Watergate cover-up and he was forced to leave office.

2. _____ Diversity is increasing in our colleges and universities. Affirmative action programs are in place at most colleges and universities.

3. _____ Chris will do extremely well in law school. He did extremely well as an undergraduate student majoring in political science.

4. _____ Violence in our schools will probably increase in the future. More and more kids are playing video games with a lot of violence in them.

5. _____ Most Americans are in favor of legalizing marijuana. A Gallup poll showed that 58% of the American people would support legalization.

6. _____ The defendant is guilty of first-degree murder. The defendant confessed to murdering the man and doing it to get revenge.

7. _____ Capital punishment discriminates against the poor. A lot of innocent people are put to death when capital punishment is used.

8. _____ The Atkins diet is as healthy as the American Heart Association Diet (AHA) is. A recent study at Duke University found that people who stayed on the Atkins diet for 6 months were just as healthy after completing the diet as were the people who stayed on the AHA diet for 6 months.

9. _____ She must be embarrassed. See, she's blushing.

10. _____ Electronic surveillance is an invasion of our privacy. One of the top legal experts in the country recently said that electronic surveillance violates our constitutional right to be left alone.

REASONING IDENTIFICATION QUIZ

Name _____   Date _____

Identify the type of reasoning used in each argument below.

1. Tom may end up getting skin cancer. He spends a lot of time out in the sun.

   Reasoning: _____

2. That restaurant must have great food. Every time I drive by, their parking lot is full!

   Reasoning: _____

3. Violence on children's television programs has increased. According to a recent report put out by the Media research Center at the University of California, violence on programs aimed at children has increased by 25% over the past 10 years.

   Reasoning: _____

4. The Washington Redskin's Robert Griffin III is one of the best quarterback's in the National Football League. Very few quarterbacks have his athletic abilities.

   Reasoning: _____

5. He's not very friendly. He hardly ever smiles.

   Reasoning: _____

6. It must be a great book. The critic gave it a great review.

   Reasoning: _____

7. It should be great going down to Florida again this year. I had a great time going down there during the break last year.

   Reasoning: _____

FALLACY MATCHING QUIZ

Name _____   Date _____

a. Begging the question   g. Red herring
b. False dilemma   h. Straw man
c. Ad hominem   i. Post hoc
d. Composition   j. Slippery slope
e. Division   f. Shifting burden of proof

_____ 1. "Euthanasia is morally acceptable. It is a decent, ethical thing to help another human being escape suffering through death."

_____ 2. Dexter: "I think that some people have psychic powers." Marion: "I doubt that?" Dexter: "No one has been able to prove that people do not have psychic powers."

_____ 3. "Senator Jones says that we should not fund the attack submarine program. I disagree entirely. I can't understand why he wants to leave us defenseless like that."

_____ 4. Person A: "I don't think young children should be allowed to play in the street." Person B: "But it would be crazy to lock them up all day with no fresh air."

_____ 5. "We've got to stop them from banning pornography. Once they start banning one form of literature, they will never stop. Next thing you know, they will be burning all the books!"

_____ 6. The picture on Jim's old TV set goes out of focus. Jim goes over and strikes the TV soundly on the side and the picture goes back into focus. Jim tells his friend that hitting the TV fixed it.

_____ 7. "Look, you are going to have to make up your mind. Either you decide that you can afford this stereo, or you decide you are going to do without music for a while."

_____ 8. Peter says, "Based on the arguments I have presented, it is obvious that it is morally wrong to use animals for food or clothing." Brian responds: "But you are wearing a leather jacket and you have a roast beef sandwich in your hand! How can you say that using animals for food and clothing is wrong!"

_____ 9. "Rita lives in a large building, so her apartment must be large."

_____ 10. "You love coffee and you love ice cream, so you have to love coffee ice cream."

Fallacy Identification Quiz

Name_____ Date_____

1. "Why do all these pro-life advocates get so worked up about fetuses when they don't seem to have the same feelings about the thousands of lives lost each year from the use of handguns."

   Fallacy_____

2. "The War in Iraq was justified. Saddam Hussein was planning to use weapons of mass destruction. To his day, No one has been able to prove that he wasn't."

   Fallacy_____

3. "Using textbooks in our schools with obscene words in them is immoral. It isn't right for our children to be exposed to uncouth and vulgar language at such an impressionable age. It's just obscene and immoral."

   Fallacy_____

4. "Ever since we quit going to church, business has been getting worse. If we want to keep from going completely bankrupt, we'd better start going back to church."

   Fallacy_____

5. "Senator Sanders says that cleaning up the environment should be our number one priority if we're going to survive the 21st century. But what does he know about this? He can't even keep his own financial affairs in order. Wasn't he indicted last month on tax evasion?"

   Fallacy_____

6. "Rick is a fine young man. Becky is a wonderful young woman. Won't they make a great couple?"

   Fallacy_____

7. "If we ban smoking in public, pretty soon we'll be banning hot dogs and cheese steaks."

   Fallacy_____

8. "I don't see how anyone can support the idea of gun control. Taking all guns away from all Americans is unfair, unworkable, and unconstitutional."

   Fallacy_____

9. "I don't think I'm going to apply to Penn State. All of the classes will have too many students. Since the University is so big, I'm sure all of the classes will be huge and impersonal."

   Fallacy_____

10. "If you can't say something nice about someone, don't say anything at all."

    Fallacy_____

Types and Tests of Evidence

Name _____   Date _____

Instructions: For each piece of evidence below, identify the *type* of evidence it is and *test* the evidence by indicating how you believe it supports the claim.

Proposition: Juvenile Offenders Should be Sentenced as Adults

1. *Juveniles old enough to know right from wrong*
   Sterling Burnett, National Center for Policy Analysis in Dallas. *Christian Science Monitor*, Aug. 18, 2010
   "Violent juveniles may not be adults but they are fully capable of committing crimes, so for society's sake, we need to keep them behind bars."

   Type _____

   Test _____

2. *Significant number of children now put in adult prisons*
   John Artis, former child prisoner put in adult prison, *Miami Herald*, July 30, 2013
   "As many as 3,500 kids are locked up in adult prisons every day."

   Type _____

   Test _____

3. *Putting minors in adult prisons turns them into career criminals*
   Rachel O'Neal, *Arkansas Democrat Gazette*, Aug. 20, 1998 (quoting Dr. Steinberg, Prof. of psychology at Temple University and Director of MacArthur Foundation Research)
   "Trying younger children as adults and putting them into adult prisons increases the likelihood that they will become more serious offenders once they are released from prison."

   Type _____

   Test _____

4. *Juveniles in adult prisons more likely than adults to commit suicide*
   Kidsinprison.com, March 19, 2013
   Juveniles are four times as likely as adults to report being assaulted in DOC facilities. They are the most likely to be victims of assault. Some attacks are at the hands of adults, others are from other kids and guards.

   Type _____

   Test _____

Proposition: The Use of Cell Phones While Driving Should be Prohibited

5. *Cell phones a major distraction*
   Brenda Rios, Detroit Free Press, 9-22-2012
   Consider the case of Jane Wagner, who was distracted by her cell phone when she hit and killed Naeun Yoon.

   Type _____

   Test _____

6. *Public believes cell phones are a distraction*
   AP online, September, 2008
   In a recent survey answered by 12,920 drivers and conducted by J.D. Power and Associates, 64% said dialing while driving is very distracting.

   Type _____

   Test _____

7. ***Cell phones are being banned in many places***

Wikipedia article on mobile phones and driving safety, 2014

Already 16 states and more than 65 foreign countries have established bans on the use of hand-held cell phones while driving, and several other states are considering similar laws.

Type _____

Test _____

Proposition: Marijuana Should be Legalized

8. ***Too much money is being spent on prosecuting marijuana users***

William F. Buckley, Public advocate, Albuquerque Journal, June 8, 2009

"The amount of money and of legal energy being given to prosecute Americans who are caught with a few ounces of marijuana in their possession makes no sense."

Type _____

Test _____

9. ***Marijuana use can damage brain cells***

Julian Bettrame, MaClean's, Aug. 6, 2011

"There are the intoxicating, disorienting effects, which some studies show have been associated with impairment and short-term memory loss. Even the most ardent advocates of pot smoking will generally admit that driving a car is not advisable under the drug's spell."

Type _____

Test _____

10. ***Marijuana use can increase heart attack risk***

Science News, 7-14-2012

There have been several instances where otherwise healthy people have suffered heart attacks shortly after smoking marijuana.

Type _____

Test _____

ANALYZING SUPPORTING EVIDENCE

Name _____   Date _____

You are preparing to give a speech arguing against the proposition that *West Chester University should seek admission to a bigger athletic conference.*

One of your main points is that "big-time" athletics is contrary to the educational aims of the University. In your research, you have gathered the evidence listed below. Which of these would you use and which would you not use? Justify your decision in each case using any relevant tests of evidence, and reasoning. Please explain answers thoroughly.

A. A statement by the president of a fraternity of the Pennsylvania State University campus: "Our house always tries to pledge two or three athletes each year for prestige purposes but we don't want too many athletes in our chapter. Big-time varsity athletes are out of it socially; most of them are downright crude."

B. A statement from the President of Hope College (enrollment 500): "Big-Time athletic programs are contrary to every principle of American democratic education. Emphasis on athletics inevitably leads to a de-emphasis on scholarship."

C. A statement from Matthew Leonard, former Pennsylvania State football star: "When I was at Penn. State which is part of the Big Ten, I was kept so busy with football practices and physical conditioning while in college that I never really had time to learn anything in my classes. Football practices and skull sessions often ran as late as 10:00 p.m. and then I was just too tired to do any lessons. I am afraid that in many cases I was given passing grades in order to insure my continued eligibility for football."

D. A quotation from an editorial in the *Saturday Evening Post*, April, 2012: "No school has ever been able to maintain a sound academic atmosphere in the face of a big-time athletic program. When the University of Chicago was in the Big Ten, it did have a truly intellectual atmosphere, but this was hardly true in any other Big Ten school."

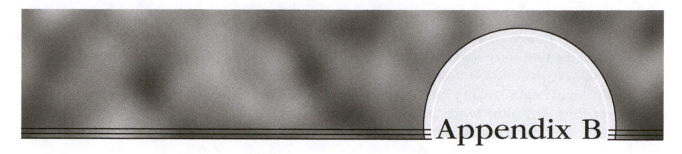

Debate Activities

IDENTIFY THE TYPE OF PROPOSITION

Name _____   Date _____

We've discussed three types of propositions: *fact, value,* and *policy*. A ***fact*** asserts the existence of past, present, or future phenomena; facts can be verified as true or false and use "neutral" terms. A ***value*** proposition asserts the worth of something; it expresses a positive or negative attitude in a judgmental way. A ***policy*** proposition states what should be done to remedy a problem that is not now being done.

   For each proposition listed below, indicate whether you think it is a proposition of *fact, value,* or *policy.*

   1. _____ Extraterrestrial beings visited Earth during prehistoric times.

   2. _____ Pennsylvania should require all teachers to pass a proficiency examination.

   3. _____ The Constitution protects the right to have an abortion.

   4. _____ Illegal immigrants generally take jobs U.S. citizens do not want.

   5. _____ Racial profiling is wrong.

   6. _____ A cure for the AIDS disease will soon be found.

   7. _____ Gun control laws would do more harm than good.

   8. _____ Polygraph evidence should be admissible in a court of law.

   9. _____ Most businesses have policies designed to prevent sexual harassment.

   10. _____ Pornography on the Internet can cause aggressive behavior in children.

   11. _____ The New York Yankees are a better baseball team than the Boston Red Sox.

   12. _____ The use of cell phones in automobiles should be prohibited.

CHOOSING A DEBATE TOPIC

Name _____   Date _____

Purpose: To identify a number of controversial topics and sources suitable for classroom debate, and to formulate different kinds of propositions for each topic.

Procedure:

1. ***Browse CQ Researcher***. Go to your library's website and do a title search for "CQ Researcher." Click on the title entry for CQ Researcher, and then click on the web link for it. When the web page appears for the CQ Researcher, click on "browse by date" (or "browse by subject if you prefer") and begin looking for a good, controversial topic.

2. ***Select four different topics***. Choose four topics you think would be good for class policy debates. For each topic you choose, briefly note why you chose it and why you think it would be a good topic for class debate.

   Topic 1 _____

   Why? _____

   _____

   Topic 2 _____

   Why? _____

   _____

   Topic 3 _____

   Why? _____

   _____

   Topic 4 _____

   Why? _____

   _____

3. ***Identify the sources***. Click on the pro/con essays for each topic you selected, identify the author of the <u>pro</u> side and the author of the <u>con</u> side as presented in CQ Researcher. Briefly note their qualifications on the topic (who are they?).

   Topic 1: Pro _____

   Topic 1: Con _____

   Topic 2: Pro _____

   Topic 2: Con _____

   Topic 3: Pro _____

   Topic 3: Con _____

   Topic 4: Pro _____

   Topic 4: Con _____

4. ***Phrase a proposition***. *For each topic, write a proposition of policy.*

   Topic 1: _____

   Topic 2: _____

   Topic 3: _____

   Topic 4: _____

5. *Write an argument*. Write a reason for (advocating) and against (opposing) each of the four propositions above.

Advocating topic 1: _____

Opposing topic 1: _____

Advocating topic 2: _____

Opposing topic 2: _____

Advocating topic 3: _____

Opposing topic 3: _____

Advocating topic 4: _____

Opposing topic 4: _____

WHO HAS THE BURDEN OF PROOF?

Name _____   Date _____

In a dispute, someone has the **burden of proof**. This means that the person must present an argument convincing enough to "overcome" the **presumption** given to his or her opponent. In formal disputes, such as those that take place in courtrooms or debating contests, presumption and burden of proof are clearly assigned to the speakers in advance (i.e., the prosecuting attorney; the affirmative speaker). In most situations, presumption depends on which speaker supports the **status quo** or which speaker subscribes to the audience's point-of-view (the latter naturally will take precedence over the former if the audience determines who prevails). In situations where the status quo favors neither side, the person who asserts a claim has the burden to offer proof of the claim.

In each of the disputes below, circle the name of the speaker you believe has the burden of proof. In the space below, indicate why you think that person has the burden of proof.

1. George: "Tom Hanks is a great actor."
   Susan: "I think he's a terrible actor."

   Explain: _____

2. Maria: "The General Education requirements here should be changed."
   Alyssa: "No. You're wrong."

   Explain: _____

3. Josh: "Global warming is a serious problem."
   Darla: "The effects of global warming are little more than media hype."

   Explain: _____

4. Kirk: "The Philadelphia Phillies will have a losing record this year."
   James: "No way. They're too good for that to happen."

   Explain: _____

5. Ron: "Exercise is a great way to reduce stress."
   Ellen: "That's a lot of nonsense."

   Explain: _____

6. Tina: "This campus is racist."
   Fred: "No it isn't."

   Explain: _____

STOCK ISSUES WORKSHEET

Please complete this form in your group and turn it in when you are done.

Name _____   Date _____

Group's Policy Proposition #1: _____

_____

Advocates: _____   Opponents: _____

                _____   _____

                _____   _____

                _____   _____

                _____   _____

Advocate's claim on significance issue: Opponent's claim on significance issue:

(*problem is significant because . . .*)   (*problem not significant because . . .*)

_____   _____

_____   _____

Advocate's claim on inherency issue: Opponent's claim on inherency issue:

(*problem inherent because . . .*)   (*problem not inherent because . . .*)

_____   _____

_____   _____

Advocate's claim on workability issue: Opponent's claim on workability issue:

(*plan will solve problem because . . .*)   (*plan won't solve problem because . . .*)

_____   _____

_____   _____

Advocate's claim on cost issue: Opponent's claim on cost issue:

(*plan's costs not significant because . . .*)   (*plan's costs are significant because . . .*)

_____   _____

_____   _____

Group's Policy Proposition #2: _____

_____

Advocates: _____   Opponents: _____

(*switch sides*)

                _____   _____

                _____   _____

                _____   _____

                _____   _____

Advocate's claim on significance issue: Opponent's claim on significance issue:

(*problem is significant because . . .*)   (*problem not significant because . . .*)

_____   _____

_____   _____

Advocate's claim on inherency issue: Opponent's claim on inherency issue:

(*problem inherent because . . .*)   (*problem not inherent because . . .*)

_____   _____

_____   _____

Advocate's claim on workability issue: Opponent's claim on workability issue:

(*plan will solve problem because . . .*)   (*plan won't solve problem because . . .*)

_____   _____

_____   _____

Advocate's claim on cost issue: Opponent's claim on cost issue:

(*plan's costs not significant because . . .*)   (*plan's costs are significant because . . .*)

_____   _____

_____   _____

RECORDING EVIDENCE

Name _____   Date _____

At this point, you need to begin finding and recording evidence that supports your contentions. Eventually, you will record each piece of evidence (supporting material such as testimony, examples, and statistics) on a 4 × 6 index card following the basic format noted below.

Top of card: Write a **claim** that lets you know what the evidence proves.

Next line: Write the **source** of the evidence, which must include the name of the author, his/her qualifications, name of the publication, and year of publication (to assess credibility of source).

The rest of the card: Write the **evidence**. For testimony, use a direct quotation. For other types of evidence, paraphrase to get the main points. Be sure to limit the material to only that which supports the heading you have on the first line.

Find a good piece of evidence that supports one of your contentions and complete these cards:

Claim: _____

Source: _____

_____

Evidence:

Claim: _____

Source: _____

_____

Evidence:

Claim: _____

Source: _____

_____

Evidence:

Claim: _____

Source: _____

_____

Evidence:

SPEECH OUTLINE WORKSHEET FOR POLICY DEBATE

Name _____ Advocate _____ Opponent _____

Introduction

Attention _____

_____

_____

Proposition _____

Operational definition (advocate's plan) _____

_____

_____

_____

CONTENTIONS WITH EVIDENCE *(Label types of evidence; Keep all contentions and subpoints less than 10 words in length)*

First Contention

I. _____

Subpoint A. _____

Support *Source:* _____

Type: *Evidence:* _____

_____ _____

_____

_____

Subpoint B. _____

Support *Source:* _____

Type: *Evidence:* _____

_____   _____

           _____

           _____

Second Contention

II. _____

Subpoint A. _____

Support *Source:* _____

Type: *Evidence:* _____

_____   _____

           _____

           _____

Subpoint B. _____

Support *Source:* _____

Type: *Evidence:* _____

_____   _____

           _____

           _____

Third Contention

III. _____

Subpoint A. _____

Support *Source:* _____

Type: *Evidence:* _____

_____   _____

           _____

           _____

Subpoint B. _____

Support *Source:* _____

Type: *Evidence:* _____

_____   _____

           _____

           _____

Conclusion

Summary of contentions

    I. _____

    II. _____

    III. _____

Attention _____

_____

_____

Bibliography of Sources

_____

_____

_____

_____

_____

_____

UNSCRAMBLE AN AFFIRMATIVE CASE OUTLINE

Name _____ Date _____

General Instructions: This exercise involves unscrambling the contentions and subpoints in an affirmative case on the proposition that *the federal government should prohibit the use of surface mining in the United States*. Enter each number (representing an argument) into its proper position so that the stock issues of harm, inherency, plan, and workability are logically presented in the order you are likely to see in a first affirmative constructive speech..

1. Surface mining causes harmful flooding.
2. Administration of this plan will be through the EPA.
3. There is significant land damage in the Eastern U.S.
4. Chemical drainage is significant.
5. Land damage cannot be controlled.
6. Surface mining causes harmful chemical drainage.
7. All surface mining of coal will be phased out within 18 months.
8. There is significant land damage in the Western U.S.
9. Flooding cannot be controlled
10. Loss of capital investment by surface mine operators will be compensated through general revenue & increased costs in coal
11. Surface Mining causes harmful land damage.
12. Flooding is significant.
13. Chemical drainage cannot be controlled.

14. Plan ensures that the harms caused by surface mining will not increase.

15. Land damage is significant.

    I. _____
        A. _____
            1. _____
            2. _____
        B. _____
    II. _____
        A. _____
        B. _____
    III. _____
        A. _____
        B. _____
Plan: _____
        A. _____
        B. _____
        C. _____
    IV. _____

UNSCRAMBLING CASE OUTLINES

Name _____   Date _____

General Instructions: This exercise involves unscrambling the contentions and subpoints in an affirmative case on the proposition that *The United States should pass a Constitutional amendment prohibiting the President from impounding funds appropriated by Congress.* It also involves matching negative arguments with the affirmative case arguments they attempt to refute.

    Part I. Directions: The following statements fit logically into the affirmative case structure (outline) provided below. Enter each number (representing an argument) into its proper position so that the stock issues of harm, inherency, plan, and workability are logically presented in the order you are likely to see in a first affirmative constructive speech..

1. One million of the poor do not receive necessary money for food and housing
2. A constitutional amendment ensures the intent of Congress is followed
3. Presidents have the power to impound funds appropriated by Congress
4. Court challenges to presidential acts of impoundment are too slow
5. A constitutional amendment disallowing impoundment
6. A constitutional amendment is a permanent change which cannot be overturned depending upon which political party is in control
7. Impoundment kills needed programs
8. Impoundment is harmful
9. Two million students do not receive money for school loans
10. Impoundment subverts democracy
11. A constitutional amendment guarantees that necessary government programs will be funded
12. Congress has no control over the President
13. Impoundment is not a veto, so Congress cannot vote to override
14. A constitutional amendment will stop U.S. presidents from impounding funds

Affirmative Case Structure	*Negative Arguments*
I. _____	_____
II. _____	_____
A. _____	_____
B. _____	_____
1. _____	_____
2. _____	_____
III. _____	_____
A. _____	_____
B. _____	_____
Plan: _____	_____
IV. _____	_____
A. _____	_____
B. _____	_____
C. _____	_____

Part II

Directions: Take the following negative arguments of refutation and place them directly across from the appropriate affirmative arguments where you would logically argue them during a negative constructive speech.

1. Show poor folks need the money
2. Courts have solved before (Kennedy law suit)
3. Show students need the money
4. Current Impoundment Control Act take power away from the U.S. President
5. Students have other ways to get money
6. There is nothing wrong with subverting democracy
7. Show poor folks cannot get money from other programs
8. Students can get scholarships
9. Plan will upset the balance of power between the three government branches
10. Students can get private loans
11. Show actual harm

STOCK ISSUES DEBATE JUDGING BALLOT

Judge _____   Date _____

Advocate _____   Opponent _____

Proposition _____

Instructions: Your job as a judge in this debate is to decide who won, based on your analysis of the *stock issues*. Briefly, if you believe the advocate met his or her *burden of proof* on the stock issues, you should vote for the advocate. However, if you believe the opponent clearly won one of the stock issues, you should vote for the opponent.

SIGNIFICANCE: Is there a significant problem today? Are many people being hurt? The advocate says yes and the opponent says no.

Who was more convincing on this issue?   Advocate _____ Opponent _____

Explain:

INHERENCY: Is the problem inherent (not being solved today)? The advocate says it isn't being solved and the opponent says it is, or can be without much change.

Who was more convincing on this issue?   Advocate _____ Opponent _____

Explain:

WORKABILITY: Can the plan/policy do a better job of solving the problem than the status quo? The advocate says yes and the opponent says no.

Who was more convincing on this issue?   Advocate _____ Opponent _____

Explain:

COST: Is the plan/policy more harmful than the status quo? The opponent says yes and the advocate says no.

Who was more convincing on this issue?   Advocate _____ Opponent _____

Explain:

Who won the debate? Advocate _____ Opponent _____

DEBATE TIMEKEEPING FORMS

DEBATE #1

Advocate _____ Opponent _____ Timer _____ Date _____

INSTRUCTIONS: Please record the time remaining for each speaker as follows:

Advocate's opening speech (5 minutes) _____

Opponent's preparation (2 minutes) _____

Opponent's cross-examination (2 minutes) _____

Opponent's preparation (continue as needed) _____

Opponent's speech (6 minutes) _____

Advocate's preparation (2 minutes) _____

Advocate's cross-examination (2 minutes) _____

Advocate's preparation (continued) _____

Advocate's rebuttal (3 minutes) _____

DEBATE #2

Advocate _____Opponent_____ Timer_____ Date_____

INSTRUCTIONS: Please record the time remaining for each speaker as follows:

Advocate's opening speech (5 minutes)	_____
Opponent's preparation (2 minutes)	_____
Opponent's cross-examination (2 minutes)	_____
Opponent's preparation (continue as needed)	_____
Opponent's speech (6 minutes)	_____
Advocate's preparation (2 minutes)	_____
Advocate's cross-examination (2 minutes)	_____
Advocate's preparation (continued)	_____
Advocate's rebuttal (3 minutes)	_____

Appendix C

Argumentation and Debate Books

BOOKS ON ARGUMENTATION

Herrick, J. A. (2011). *Argumentation: Understanding and shaping arguments.* State College, PA: Strata.

Hollihan, T. A., & Baaske, K. (2005). *Arguments and arguing: The products and process of human decision making.* Long Grove, IL: Waveland.

Inch, E. S., Warnick, B., & Endres, D. (2006). *Critical thinking and communication: The use of reason in argument.* Boston, MA: Allyn & Bacon.

Johnson, R. H., & Anthony Blair, J. (2006). *Logical self-defense.* New York, NY: International Debate Education Association.

Kahane, H., & Cavender, N. *Logic and contemporary rhetoric: The use of reason in everyday life.* Belmont, CA: Wadswoth.

Makau, J. (1988). *Reasoning and communication: Thinking critically about arguments.* Belmont, CA: Wadsworth.

Munson, R., & Black, A. (2006). *The elements of reason.* Belmont, CA: Wadsworth.

Rieke, R. D., Sillars, M. O., & Peterson, T. R. (2012). *Argumentation and the decision making process.* Boston, MA: Pearson.

Rybacki, K. C., & Rybacki, D. J. (2011). *Advocacy and opposition: An introduction to argumentation.* Boston, MA: Pearson

Schiappa, E., & Nordin, J. (2013). *Argumentation: Keeping faith with reason.* Boston, MA: Pearson.

Toulmin, S. (1958). *The uses of argument.* Cambridge, UK: Cambridge University Press.

VerLinden, J. (2005). *Critical thinking and everyday argument.* Belmont, CA: Wadsworth.

Walton, D. (2013). *Methods of argumentation.* Cambridge, UK: Cambridge University Press.

BOOKS ON DEBATE

Bartanen, M., & Frank, D. A. (2001). *Lincoln-Douglas debate: Preparing for value argumentation.* New York, NY: McGraw-Hill.

Corcoran, J. M., Nelson, M., & Perella, J. (2012). *Critical thinking through debate.* Dubuque, IA: Kendall Hunt.

Edwards, R. E. (2008). *Competitive debate: The official guide.* New York, NY: Alpha.

Freeley, A. J., & Steinberg, D. L. (2013). *Argumentation and debate*. New York, NY: Cengage.

Knapp, T. G., & Galizio, L. A. (1999). *Elements of parliamentary debate: A guide to public argument*. New York, NY: Longman.

Leigh, M. G. (2005). *The approachable argument*. Dubuque, IA: Kendall Hunt.

Meany, J., & Shuster, K. (2008). *On that point: An introduction to parliamentary debate*. New York, NY: International Debate Education Association.

Snider, A., & Schnurer, M. (2002). *Many sides: Debate across the curriculum*. New York, NY: International Debate Education Association.

Ziegelmueller, G. W., & Kay, J. (1997). *Argumentation: Inquiry and advocacy*. Boston, MA: Allyn & Bacon.

Glossary

Academic Debate—An invention of educational institutions that allows students to present and refute arguments from an opposing team or an individual student on a specific topic in a structured setting. The format has a set order and number of timed speeches to make the debating process equitable to both sides (chapter 8).

Ad Hominem—A fallacy of attacking an opponent's character instead of disputing the opponent's arguments on an issue (chapter 3).

Ad Populum—A fallacy of assuming that something is true or good merely because most people believe it to be true or good (also called the bandwagon fallacy) (chapter 3).

Affirmative Case—The case constructed by an advocate supporting the proposition in policy or value debate (chapter 6).

American Forensics Association (AFA)—AFA is a professional collegiate academic association which sponsors the annual National Debate Tournament (NDT) hosted by a different college each year since 1967. The membership of this association consists of communication professors, collegiate debate and forensics coaches (chapter 8).

Argumentation—Explicit or implicit messages that are supported with evidence and reasoning; argumentation consists of two components: the claim and the proof (chapter 1).

Appeal to Ignorance—A fallacy that attempts to escape the burden of proof by giving it to one's adversary. Also referred to as shifting the burden of proof (chapter 3).

Applied Debate—Addresses propositions in which the advocates have a special interest, and the debate takes place before a judge or an audience with the power to render a binding decision. These debates occur in a variety of formats usually decided by the group or organization sponsoring the event (chapter 8).

Attack Ad—Advertisement that creates a negative image of the opposing candidate by distorting his or her image and record, taking quotations out of context, making ad hominem attacks, and using guilt by association (chapter 9).

Audience Analysis—Discovering vital information about an audience in order to adapt a specific message to meet the needs of the audience (chapter 1).

Backing—Part of an argument in the Toulmin model that provides support for the warrant (reasoning) (chapter 2).

Begging the Question—A fallacy based on the false assumption that a given premise supports a claim when in fact there is little substantive difference between the premise and the claim (chapter 3).

Beyond a Reasonable Doubt—The argument is so convincing, a reasonable person would accept it without hesitation; thus the proposition was proven without a "reasonable doubt" (see also Burden of proof) (chapter 9).

Bias—Test of evidence that evaluates the self-interests of the source in relation to the information that is reported (chapter 4).

Brainstorming—The process whereby new, different, or original ideas are generated. When starting work on a debate proposition, generating ideas is essential. To brainstorm, let your mind wander to consider all possible interpretations, issues, principles, and arguments relevant to the topic (chapter 6).

Burden of Clash—The obligation of each side in a debate to respond directly to the arguments of the other side (chapter 7).

Burden of Proof—The obligation to initiate debate by offering convincing arguments in favor of the proposition (chapter 5).

Burden of Rejoinder—The obligation to present convincing counter-arguments in response to a prima facie case for a proposition (chapter 5).

CEDA—In 1971, the Cross Examination Debate Association (CEDA) was created to provide an alternative to National Debate Tournament debating—in part to meet a perceived need by placing greater emphasis on communication (chapter 8).

Claim—A statement of belief; that part of an argument directly supported by the premise (grounds) and the reasoning (warrant) in the argument (chapters 1 and 2).

Common Law—Originates from past judicial decisions. These legal parameters guide judges in rendering decisions and/or instructing the jury how to apply the law to their decisions; the system also guides judges in determining if a case has been properly brought before the court, if a *prima facie* case has been established, and if evidence has been properly admitted (chapter 9).

Comparative Advantages Case—An organizational structure demonstrating that the affirmative plan achieves an improvement over the status quo. The advocates are not claiming to solve the entire problem—only that they have a better, more advantageous policy than that of the status quo (chapter 6).

Completeness—A test of evidence that evaluates whether the source (or the evidence provided in the argument) provides enough information for a reasonable person to accept (chapter 4).

Conceptual Definition—The words, phrases, or statements that define the terms contained in a proposition (chapter 5).

Consistency—A test of evidence that evaluates whether there are contradictions contained in the same source (chapter 4).

Constitutional Law—Laws that are created and written by the legislative branch of the federal, state, or local government (chapter 9).

Constructive Speech—The opening speech of each debater that presents their own case for or against the proposition (chapter 7).

Contention—A term that describes the primary arguments in your case. Most cases will have between 3 and 5 major arguments or contentions (chapter 6).

Contract Debates—From 1920 to 1946, a college debating team would send out contracts to teams from other schools requesting an opportunity to debate. The contract would specify details such as which team would argue what side of the proposition, the length and number of speeches, and how to select judges (chapter 8).

Core Value—A term used when debating a value proposition that represents the key value, which becomes the standard of judgment for deciding the outcome of the debate. The core value is the standard argued to be of greatest importance when trying to decide the truth of the value judgment (chapter 6).

Corroboration—A test of evidence that evaluates whether other credible and reliable sources agree with the source's claims and the source's evidence (chapter 4).

Cost—One of the stock issues on a policy proposition that requires the advocate to prove that any costs (or disadvantages) of the plan are outweighed by its benefits (i.e., removing or lessening a significant problem) (chapter 5).

Counter Plan—A counter plan is the negative team's plan for dealing with the problem or providing the advantage identified in the affirmative case in a policy debate. When presenting a counter plan, the negative side admits there is a need to change the status quo but claims there is a better way than the affirmative plan (chapter 6).

Counterclaim—A claim presented in a debate that directly contradicts the claim of an opposing argument (chapter 7).

Credibility—A test of evidence to determine the authenticity of the source. Does the source have the background, knowledge, expertise, and integrity (ethics) to produce the information that was obtained (chapter 4).

Criteria—One of the general issues in a debate that specifies what the advocate must prove in order to establish a prima facie case for a proposition (i.e., the standards for determining the burden of proof) (chapter 5).

Criteria Case—This type of affirmative case focuses on the characteristics or criteria upon which policy alternatives should be based. This strategy highlights the requirements of an ideal policy and then constructs a plan that meets those standards (chapter 6).

Critical Thinking—The ability to carefully and deliberately evaluate the logical relationships among ideas, claims, and arguments to judge their validity and/or worth (chapter 1).

Cross-Examination—The brief period in a debate that gives debaters an opportunity to question the other side as a way of weakening opposing arguments and strengthening their own (chapter 7).

Culture—The traditions, beliefs, values, and practices that are passed down from generation to generation (chapter 1).

Cultural Belief—What a majority of individuals in a culture believe is true (chapter 1).

Currency—A test of evidence that evaluates the recency of information (chapter 4).

Database—An organized collection of information that can be accessed electronically (chapter 4).

Debate—A formal method of presenting arguments for and against a proposition (chapter 1).

Deductive Argument—The claim must follow from the premises. That is, if we accept the premises, we have to accept the claim. It is a logical necessity (chapter 2).

Delivery—The nonverbal behavior of the speaker that carries the spoken message, including his or her physical appearance, eye contact, posture, positioning, gestures, facial expressions, and tone of voice (chapter 7).

Demographics—The characteristics of the audience such as (but are not limited to): culture, ethnicity, gender, age, educational level, economic status, religious beliefs, political identification, and marital status (chapter 1).

Direct Speech—Speech that promotes an interpersonal connection with the audience (e.g., eye contact, close proximity) (chapter 7).

Discovery Period—In the legal field where both sides can request to review the evidence and documents related to the case (chapter 9).

Disputations—Highly structured discussions of logical questions that became popular during the 19th century (chapter 8).

Dynamic Speech—Forceful, energetic, and animated speech that conveys to an audience the impression that a speaker cares deeply about the points he or she is trying to get across (chapter 7).

Ethos—The audience's perception of the speaker's source credibility that consists of elements such as the speaker's character, integrity, knowledge, and competence (chapter 1).

Evidence—External data (supporting material) that proves a point (chapter 4).

Evidence Card—An index card that contains support for the arguments in your case. To create these cards, you need to write down specific facts and opinions from the sources you have collected in an organized system, which will allow you to find what you need when you are ready to construct your case (chapter 6).

Examples—Specific cases that support a claim (chapter 4).

Expert Testimony—When an individual is widely recognized as a credible source of knowledge and whose opinion is acknowledged as having authority in his or her field (chapter 9).

Extemporaneous Speaking—Planning and preparing a speech ahead of time and delivering the speech from an outline or notes (chapter 1).

Extending an Argument—Responding directly to the argument of a previous speaker in a way that advances debate on that argument (chapter 7).

Facts—Information we can verify to be true (chapter 4).

Fallacy—A defective argument based on an error in reasoning and/or an attempt to mislead (chapter 3).

Fallacy of Composition—Assuming that what is true of the parts must be true of the whole (chapter 3).

Fallacy of Division—Assumes that what is true of the whole must be true of the parts (chapter 3).

False Dilemma—Sometimes called the "either-or" fallacy, this defective argument occurs when the reasoning in an argument assumes the existence of only two alternatives, when in fact there are more than two (i.e., a false dichotomy) (chapter 3).

Fields of Argument—Argumentation within professional contexts where policy making institutions use argumentation and debate to create policies that directly impact how we live, how we consume material goods, and how we are governed (chapter 9).

Fluent Speech—Speech that is free of extraneous pauses and hesitations (chapter 7).

Flow Sheet—A note-taking method used in debates in which a sheet of paper is divided into columns, with each column showing the arguments presented in a particular speech (chapter 7).

Formal Fallacy—A flawed deductive argument (chapter 3).

Goals Case—This type of affirmative case advocates a new plan to meet status quo goals, which are currently not being realized. The affirmative must identify, state, and accept the goals that were established by the past or current lawmakers and then argue that these goals would be better met through the affirmative plan (chapter 6).

Grounds—Part of an argument in the Toulmin model that provides direct support for the claim (also referred to as the premise) (chapter 2).

Identification—When the speaker creates a common bond with the audience (chapter 1).

Independent Arguments—Arguments containing multiple premises in which each premise offers a sufficient reason for accepting the claim (chapter 2).

Inductive Argument—An argument in which the claim is based on some degree of probability (truth) rather than on logical necessity (validity) (chapter 2).

Informal Fallacy—A flawed inductive argument (chapter 3).

Inherency—The stock issue on a policy proposition that requires the advocate to prove that the status quo (i.e., present policies) is not capable of meeting the need for change identified the advocate (chapter 5).

Intelligible Speech—Speech that is clear and comprehensible (chapter 7).

Interdependent Arguments—Arguments containing multiple premises in which none of the premises alone are sufficient to support the claim (chapter 2).

Issues—Important questions that frame key points of disagreement (chapter 5).

Judging Paradigm—The model the judge uses to evaluate the debate round. This model illustrates how judges view debates by identifying which types of issues will be prioritized in terms of the way a judge will cast a decision at the end of a debate (chapter 8).

Lay Judges—Judges who do not have any background or very limited background in debate (chapter 8).

Lincoln–Douglas (LD) Debate—A type of debate format in which one debater argues against another individual (rather than a two-person team). This style originated from the famous debates between Stephen A. Douglas and Abraham Lincoln in their race for the U.S. Senate during 1858 (chapter 8).

Logos—Reasoning; the logical use of reasoning in argumentation to persuade an audience (chapter 1).

Maslow's Hierarchy of Needs—The idea that individuals have specific desires and wants, which are arranged hierarchically and must be satisfied; these needs include: physical needs, safety needs, belonging and love needs, esteem needs, and self-actualization (chapter 1).

Minor Repair—An argumentation strategy available to the negative side in policy debate. It involves the negative team contending that a small alteration in the status quo is as effective as the affirmative plan, but requires substantially less change than that proposed by the affirmative, which makes it a better policy alternative (chapter 6).

National Forensics Association—A professional collegiate organization. Currently, the National Forensic Association at the collegiate level regulates LD debate (chapter 8).

Narratives—A type of evidence in which stories are used to make a logical point (chapter 4).

NDT Debate—Stands for the national debate tournament (the oldest championship tournament for college debate); these initials are also synonymous with the competitive style of collegiate policy debate represented at tournaments held throughout the academic year (chapter 8).

Need-Plan Case—A type of affirmative case, which uses a problem solution organizational structure. The affirmative side identifies a significant problem, indicates why the status quo cannot or will not solve the problem, and proposes a workable solution (chapter 6).

Negative Campaign—Argumentation that focuses on the negative aspects of a candidate or policy to smear an opposing candidate (chapter 9).

Negative Case—A set of arguments put together by an opponent of the proposition in policy or value debate. In policy debate, it can involve direct refutation, a minor repair and/or a counter plan (chapter 6).

Non sequitur—Any argument containing a claim that does not follow from the premises (chapter 3).

Operational definition—The plan of action offered by the advocate of a policy proposition (chapter 5).

Parliamentary Debate—An academic debate format that is closely modeled after the Oxford Union Debate practiced in British colleges and is less structured than other debate formats. This form of debate may use fact, value, or policy propositions and allows for greater audience involvement (chapter 8).

Pathos—Emotion; the use of emotional appeals in argumentation to persuade an audience (chapter 1).

Plan—The specific proposal offered by an advocate of a policy proposition; presented as an operational definition of the policy proposition (chapter 5).

Point of Information—Used in parliamentary debate as an alternative to cross-examination. After the first minute and before the last minute of all constructive speeches, the opposing team may offer points of information to the speaker who holds the floor. The purpose of these statements or questions is to clarify a point the speaker is making, advance a point for the opposing team, or highlight a weakness in the other team's case (chapter 8).

Point of Order—A question directed to the judge in a parliamentary debate about a possible rule violation of an opposing speaker. The judge must make an immediate ruling and does not need to justify the decision he or she makes (chapter 8).

Policymaker Judge—A debate judge that evaluates the affirmative's policy system compared to the negative's policy system (a defense of the status quo, a minor repair, a counter plan) and then makes a decision as to whether or not the affirmative offers a better policy option (chapter 8).

Post Hoc Fallacy—Assuming that one event (A) causes another event (B), simply because (A) precedes (B) (chapter 3).

Preponderance of the Evidence—The argument presents enough evidence that the fact or facts is more likely than not (chapter 9).

Presumption—A bias in favor of claims that support the status quo (chapter 5).

Prima facie Case—A set of arguments sufficient "on its first appearance" to convince a reasonable person that the proposition is probably true (chapter 5).

Primary Source—A type of evidence that includes documents, physical objects, original works, or eyewitness accounts that were created during the actual historical time period that is being examined (chapter 4).

Proof—The evidence and reasoning that support a claim; proof represents the second component of argumentation (chapter 1).

Proposition—A statement of belief (claim) put to debate (chapter 5).

Proposition of Fact—A claim that asserts the existence of something in the past, present, or future (chapter 5).

Proposition of Value—A claim that asserts the relative worth of something; it recommends a plan of action (i.e., policy) (chapter 5).

Proposition of Policy—A claim that asserts that something should be done (chapter 5).

Qualifier—Part of the Toulmin model of argument that indicates how certain the arguer is that the claim is true (chapter 2).

Reasoning—How the premise in an argument provides support for the claim in the argument (chapter 2).

Reasoning by Analogy—Bases the truth of a claim on a comparison between two things, asserting that what is true of one is most likely true of the other. Implicit in this type of reasoning is the assumption that the similarities between the two things are more telling than are the differences (chapter 2).

Reasoning by Authority—Bases the truth of a claim on the credibility of an external source (chapter 2).

Reasoning by Cause—Bases the truth of a claim on a cause–effect relationship between two things, one leading to the other. In this type of argument, the claim identifies the effect (consequent) and the grounds (premise) implicate the cause (antecedent) (chapter 2).

Reasoning by Definition—Bases the truth of a claim on the essential features or nature of something. Implicit in this type of reasoning is some criteria on which to draw an interpretation or render a judgment (chapter 2).

Reasoning by Generalization—Bases the truth of a claim on one or more typical cases, arguing that what is true of some cases is probably true of most cases (chapter 2).

Reasoning by Sign—Bases the truth of a claim on a relationship between two things where one indicates the other. In this type of argument, the indicator (or sign) appears in the grounds (premise), while the thing indicated by the sign appears in the claim (chapter 2).

Rebuttal7—A speech in a debate that gives each side an opportunity to extend and refute the arguments presented in constructive speeches (chapter 7).

Red Herring—The fallacy of introducing an irrelevant claim in order to divert attention away from the real issue (chapter 3).

Refutation—The act of disputing an opposing argument by directly challenging the claim, the premise, and/or the reasoning of the argument (chapter 7).

Reservation—That part of the Toulmin model of argument that represents a likely counterpoint to the argument (also called the rebuttal) (chapter 2).

Rhetoric—The use of symbols (verbal and nonverbal) to influence others (chapter 1).

Secondary Source—A type of evidence (a document) that was created after the actual time period that is being examined (chapter 4).

Skills Judge—A debate judge that focuses on the skills listed on a debate ballot: analysis, reasoning, evidence, organization, refutation, delivery, and cross-examination, and carefully evaluates which team has performed better with regard to each of these skills (chapter 8).

Slippery Slope—Assuming that one event will trigger an unavoidable series of events that eventually produce a horrific result (chapter 3).

Significance—The stock issue in a policy debate that requires an advocate to prove there is a "significant need" to change, such as solving a problem that is hurting many people, and/or draining highly valued resource (chapter 5).

Signposting—Words and phrases that let the audience know the speaker is moving on to another point (chapter 7).

Speech Anxiety—The specific fear of giving a speech in front of a potentially disapproving audience (chapter 7).

Stage Fright—The mental and physical manifestations of the fear associated with a public performance (chapter 7).

Statistics—Numbers used to represent information (chapter 4).

Status Quo—The set of beliefs, values, and policies currently in place (chapter 5).

Statutory Law—Laws that are created and written by the legislative branch of the federal, state, or local government (chapter 9).

Stock Issues—A set of questions that must be answered as the advocate builds a prima facie case for a proposition (chapter 5).

Stock Issues Judge—A debate judge that emphasizes stock issues of harm, inherency, workability, and cost. In order to win, the affirmative side has to win all the stock issues, but the negative needs to win only one stock issue. The affirmative is not required to win every argument in the debate, but must win each stock issue (chapter 8).

Straw Man Fallacy—A diversionary tactic of disputing a weak or defenseless claim rather than a strong and well-supported claim against one's position (chapter 3).

Syllogism—The form of a deductive argument, consisting of a major premise, minor premise, and claim (chapter 2).

Testimony—Opinion that is expressed as a direct quotation (chapter 4).

Tertiary Source—A type of evidence that compiles, summarizes, reports, or lists information from other sources (chapter 4).

Tests of Evidence—Verifying the accuracy and authenticity of evidence in order to use it as support for an argument. Tests evidence includes (but is not limited to): credibility, bias, consistency, completeness, and corroboration (chapter 4).

Topicality—The question of whether the advocate's definition of a proposition offers a correct or reasonable interpretation of the proposition (topic) chosen for debate (chapter 5).

Topicality Arguments—Strategies for debating different interpretations of the proposition (debate topic) because words in a proposition may be defined differently by opposing teams (chapter 6).

Toulmin Model—British philosopher Stephen Toulmin's model of an argument, consisting of the claim, grounds, warrant, backing, reservation, and qualifier (chapter 2).

Transition—Words, phrases, and statements that create a "bridge" from one point in a speech to another point in the speech (chapter 7).

Unobtrusive Speech—Speech that is free of distracting movements, expressions, and sounds, such as shuffling your feet, tapping your fingers, touching your face or hair, pacing back and forth, swaying from side to side, speaking too loud, mispronouncing words, sighing, smiling nervously, and so on (chapter 7).

Value Hierarchy—Shows the relative importance of different values, how they "stack up" or are "measured" against each other. When debating a value proposition, this is the critical process of explaining and defending why the value advocated by one side takes precedence over all other possible values implicit in the proposition (chapter 6).

Warrant—Part of an argument in the Toulmin model that indicates how the grounds (premise) in the argument support the claim (chapter 2).

Workability—A stock issue on a policy proposition that requires the advocate to prove that the plan being proposed can do a better job of meeting the need than the status quo can (chapter 5).

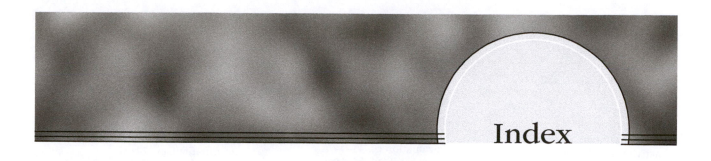

Index

Need-plan case, 68
Negative campaign, 107
Negative case, 59
  constructing, 71–74
New England Journal of
  Medicine, 40
New terms, 52
Non sequitur, 24, 25

O

Off-case arguments, 82
Online research, 40–41
Operational definition, 56
Opposing side, cross-examining,
  83–85
Oral argument, structuring,
  80–81
Oxford Union Debate, 91, 92

P

Parliamentary debate, 91–93
Pathos, 5
Person, attacking, 30
Personal growth, 6
Philadelphia Inquirer, 18, 35
Physical evidence, 101
Physical needs, 10
Plan, 56
  counter, 72–73
Point-by-point refutation, 83
Point of information, 92
Point of order, 92
Policy, proposition of, 50
  constructing cases on, 67–74
  stock issues for, 56–57
Policymaker judge, 95
Politics
  argumentation in, 104–107
  decision makers in, 104–105
Post hoc fallacy, 27
Prejudice, appealing to, 31
Preponderance of evidence, 100
Presumption, 50–51
Prima facie case, 50
Primary source, 18, 38
Professional growth, 6
Proof, 2
  burden of, shifting, 29
Propositions
  analyzing, 47–58
  debate
    advocacy and, 50–51
    general analysis of, 51–54
    nature of, 48–49
    specific analysis of, 54–57
    types of, 49–50
  of fact, 49–50
    stock issues for, 54–55
  of policy, 50

constructing cases on, 67–74
  stock issues for, 56–57
of value, 50
  advocating, 65–66
  constructing cases on, 65–67
  opposing, 66–67
  stock issues for, 55–56
Public debate, 93
Public speaking perspective,
  on argumentation, 6–8

Q

Qualifier, 16

R

Reasoning, 14
  by analogy, 19–20
  by authority, 18, 104
  by cause, 20, 103
  circular, 25–26
  by definition, 18–19
  effect-to-cause, 20
  by generalization, 19
  by sign, 20–21, 103
Rebuttal, 16, 82
Red herring, 30
Refutation, 83
  point-by-point, 83
Reservation, 16
Rhetoric, defined, 4
Rhetorical contexts, classification
  of, 4–5
Robert's Rules of Order, 3

S

Safety needs, 10
Secondary source, 18, 38–39
Self-actualization, 10
Sign, reasoning by, 20–21, 103
Significance, 56
Signposting, 81
Situational factors, 10
Skills judge, 95
Slippery slope, 28
Solvency, 57
Source citation, 44
Speech
  anxiety. *See* Speech anxiety
  constructive, 82
  deliberative, 4
  delivering, 78–81
  direct, 79, 80
  dynamic, 79, 80
  epideictic, 4
  fluent, 79, 80
  forensic, 4
  intelligible, 79, 80
  unobtrusive, 79, 80
Speech anxiety

causes of, 76–77
  managing, 76–78
    techniques for, 77–78
  symptoms of, 76–77
Stage fright, 76
Statistics, 34–35, 103
Status quo, 49
Statutory law, 100
Stock issues, 51–52
  judge, 95
  for proposition of fact, 54–55
  for proposition of policy, 56–57
  for proposition of value, 55–56
Straw man fallacy, 30
Syllogism, 14–15
  categorical, 15, 101
  disjunctive, 15
  hypothetical, 15–16
Symbols, 4

T

Technical terms, 52
Terms
  coined, 52
  defining, 52–53, 60
  equivocal, 52
  new, 52
  technical, 52
  vague, 52
Tertiary source, 39
Testimony, 104
  expert, 36, 101
  lay, 36
Tests of evidence, 41–43
  for cultural beliefs, 44
  for web pages, 43–44
Topicality, 53
Topicality arguments, 60
Torture, 52–53
Toulmin Model of Argument,
  3, 16, 18
Toulmin, Stephen, 3, 16
Tournament debates, 88–99
  judging, 93–96
Transition, 81

U

Unobtrusive speech, 79, 80

V

Vague terms, 52
Value
  core, 65
  criteria, 66, 67
  hierarchy, 66
  object, 50, 55
  proposition of, 50
    advocating, 65–66
    constructing cases on, 65–67